Hospitality Industry Profit Planning and Decision Making Techniques

Charles L. Ilvento

Florida International University

KENDALL/HUNT PUBLISHING COMPANY
4050 Westmark Drive   Dubuque, Iowa 52002

Copyright © 1996 by Kendall/Hunt Publishing Company

ISBN: 0-7872-2432-4

All rights reserved. No part of this publication may be reproduced, stored in a retrieval system, or transmitted, in any form or by any means, electronic, mechanical, photocopying, recording, or otherwise, without the prior written permission of the copyright owner.

Printed in the United States of America
10 9 8 7 6 5 4 3 2 1

Contents

Introduction v
Cover Letter vii

Case Study: Star Motel 1

		Instruction	Solution
Section 1	Summary of Initial Findings	26	26
Section 2	Ratio Analysis	28	28
	Summary Analysis of All the Ratios	36	36
Section 3	Room Demand: Area Occupancy Percentage	42	43
Section 4	Competitive Position	46	46
Section 5	Room Occupancy Forecast	50	50
Section 6	Star Motel Characterisitcs	54	54
Section 7	Marketing Plan and Competitive Position	58	58
Section 8	Timetable for Implementation—1996	62	62
Section 9	Pro-Forma Comparative Statements of Operations 1995–1996	66	
Section 10	Pro-Forma Balance Sheet	76	78
	Statement of Cash Receipts and Disbursements	76	79
	"Quick Cash Flow" Statement	77	79
Section 11	Pro-Forma Statements of Cash Receipts and Disbursements By Month	82	
Section 12	Quick Cash Flow Projections	86	86
Section 13	Analysis of Pro-Forma Statements	88	88
Section 14	Capital Expenditures	92	92
Section 15	Projected 5 Year Statement of Income	97	98
Section 16	Conclusion	102	102

INTRODUCTION

The user of this text will assume the role of the newly hired general manager arriving on the hotel premises. This is a five year old established 200 room full service motel.

The text provides information historic, present and projected for this motel, its competition and demographic data.

Questions, findings, solutions and conclusions for the first three weeks on the job as general manager of this five year old established motel is your focus.

The user is urged to use his or her own assumptions based on reading the material and their life experience. Form your own conclusions following the examples as a quide.

Reference to industry standards and examples of selected industry data has been placed within the text to aid the user in comparision analysis.

Economic studies are published monthly and annually by various hospitality industry companies and are available to the general manager.

The Star Motel text is to be used as an example and guide for successful job performance.

The general manager should set up a weekly assignment schedule to keep up to date and conduct his overall evaluation of the property, staff, and customers at present and projected.

Example:

GENERAL MANAGER SCHEDULE

Week	Day	Report Section
I	1	1
I	2	2
I	2	3
I	3	4
I	4	5
I	5	6
II	1	7
II	2	8
II	3,4	9
II	3,4	10
II	3,4	11
II	3,4	12
III	1,2	13
III	2	14
III	3	15
III	3,4	16

COVER LETTER

You as general manager will be asked to prepare a cover letter to be included with the final report to be submitted to the owners of the corporation. It should include:

1. A brief description of what you did your first month on the job as new general manager.

2. A thank you for the corporation and commitment of the employees.

3. Your major recommendations.
   A. Description of the findings.
   B. Suggested solutions.
   C. Timetable of implementation and additional costs not included in the normal operating budget(s).

4. Refer to the summary and conclusive following the letter (which is section 16).

5. Concluding statement of appreciaton.

Case Study
Star Motel

★ Purpose

Star Motel can be used in a number of ways. The user **assumes the role of general manager** and makes decisions, judgements, and projections based on the given set of given conditions and circumstances, which offer a wide range of interpretation. The user has the option of making decisions and situations based on time available, imagination, and areas in which he or she wants to concentrate.

★ Star Motel—Case Study

The Star Motel Corporation is one of four motels which are owned by Heckler Corporation. The Star Motel has never been involved in comprehensive marketing, accounting, profit planning or control. The Star Motel was incorporated and began business January 1, 1991. Recently, the Star has been "losing ground" with respect to its competitors in the industry. In short, the owners of Heckler Corporation have only recently been concerned with the Star's downward trend. This has prompted a determined effort to reverse the situation.

As the new general manager, Heckler Corporation has approached you for ideas and suggestions. After your initial meetings with the staff, it is evident that the property is in the "red." All the records are chaotic and incomplete. The financial data presented, was obtained from the outside accounting firm. Due to the absence of data, you as general manager will have to make certain assumptions which you should state clearly.

You can make your own recommendations and many arbitrary decisions based on sound judgement, expertise, evaluation and trends in the hospitality industry which are applicable to the Star Motel's competitive area. All the information you have for this task is contained herein.

Stick with the major objectives of the task. You are not to be concerned with insignificant details such as pinpointing the exact location of the motel, demographic studies of the clientele, etc.

The date you are starting as general manager is as of January 1, 1996. For the practical purposes, assume your business plan is completed over the period January 1 to 25, 1996, with your proposal and presentation to the owners and board of directors January 28, 1996. You can implement the approved changes starting February 1, 1996, however you can make operational changes from your first day on the job.

Financial Information

Attached is the last three years financial information for the Star Motel. Monthly financial data is not available.

Physical Plan

A ground floor physical plan is attached for Star Motel. The original detailed plans cannot be located.

General Information

1. **Location**: Along a major interstate highway exit just outside a city with a population of 50,000. (assume local city and state liquor and other laws.)
2. Facilities: 200 rooms, 100 seat dining room (14 sq. ft./ person), 3 meeting rooms 20, 30, and 50 seats (10 sq. ft./person), and a 75 seat bar and lounge (1500 sq. ft.), a 200 seat banquet room (2200 sq. ft.), pool, telephone service, air conditioning, and color television are also available to SM guests.

3. Store rental income is received at a rate of $30 per sq. ft. and the rooms are adjacent to the banquet area.
4. Store rental units could be converted to separate, private dining rooms for $24,000 per unit. Additional furniture, etc., would cost $30,000 in total or $9000 each for store #1, and store #2, and $12,000 for store #3.
5. The additional cost to combine the three (3) store units into a 100 seat meeting room or 90 seat banquet facility would be an additional $18,000 for removal of two walls, $9,000 ea. between #1 and #2; and #2 and #3. Additional "sound proof" panels for a center room divider cost $12,000 each.
6. To convert store rental into the present banquet facility an additional $18,000 for wall removal between #3 and banquet room, including finishing. Additionally, a room divider costs $12,000.
7. To adequately serve a banquet customer, a yardstick of 11 sq. ft. per person is used.
8. The present meeting rooms are to remain intact during 1996. The board of directors advised you that they will not approve any capital improvements during your first six months of employment.
9. Cost of an addition to the building for banquet facilities is estimated at $270 per sq. ft. Additional furniture, etc. would be $300 per seat.
10. Table settings—CGS (china, glass, and silver) now cost $120; quality settings would cost $180 per setting. (This is based on the need for three complete place settings per seat at a unit cost of $40 to $60 per single place setting.)

★ Star Motel vs. Competition

1. Star Motel—200 rooms available, opened January 1, 1991

Star Motel—200 rooms	1993	1994	1995
Average room rate	$42	$45	$42
Percentage of occupancy	90%	75%	60%
Double occupancy	40%	40%	40%

2. Bay's Inn—100 rooms available—Opened July 1, 1994

Bay's Inn—100 rooms	1994* (6 months' operation)	1995
Average room rate	$30	$30
Percentage of occupancy	80%	90%
Room revenue	$405,000	$990,000

On July 1, 1994, Bay's Inn, a budget hotel, opened at the same exit where Star Motel is located. It has 100 rooms, no restaurant, no bar operation, and no meeting space, but does have telephone service and color televisions with remote control.

3. Holinite Inn—150 rooms

There is a new 150 room Holinite Inn, a full service motel, under construction at SM's exit. It has a 100 seat dining room, 40 seat lounge, and a 300 seat banquet facility which can be divided into three individual rooms. It is scheduled to open January 1, 1997 next year. There are no other motels in the immediate area.

4. Other Competition

There is no significant competition in the market area. There are small national chain motels located 20 miles north and 20 miles south of SM's exit, which are not to be considered competitors for this analysis.

★ Demographic and Area Data
Limited Data Available
1. Industrial Park

A new Industrial Park about two miles to the west, is being developed which will increase the town's population by 10% once it is fully developed. The town's Chamber of Commerce projects an additional 200

---
*For 6 months

room demand per week will be created due to the new Industrial Park. They also project an additional demand of 10 meetings per week for 20-50 persons. A three year phase-in beginning January 1, 1997 is anticipated.

Assume:
As of July 1, 1997—The industrial park will be 33.3% occupied.
As of July 1, 1998—The industrial park will be 66.6% occupied.
As of July 1, 1999—The industrial park will be 100% occupied.

2. Research Center

A major corporation is developing a 500 employee research center approximately one mile west, to be completed in three years, to open January 1, 1999. Projected research center room demand is expected to be 100 rooms per week. A representative from the center is in the area and is seeking a fixed contract for room rates. The center will have employee and executive dining rooms and meeting facilities; however, an additional demand for two daytime meeting facilities per week for 80 to 100 persons is foreseeable. They also plan to have two banquets per month for an estimated average of 240 persons each, but want a room which accommodates 300 people.

3. Local Business

Local business, other than above, has seminar and meeting room demand estimated at: 10-20 people two times a week; 30 to 40 people two times a week; and 50 people once a week. This was for 1995 and the number of meetings can be expected to increase at a rate of 10% a year in the foreseeable future.

4. Area Room Demand

The department of Transportation and Chamber of Commerce provided the following information:

Provided from highway traffic:
1993—90 rms/day
1994—100 rms/day
1995—110 rms/days

Provided from local demand:
1993—70 rms/day
1994—80 rms/day
1995—90 rms/day

5. Other Sources

Room sales from other sources (about 20 rooms from local business visitors) is expected to increase at the rate of 10% a year in the foreseeable future.

6. Food statistics 1995:

		Dining Room			
Daily	Average Check	Hotel Guest	Non-Hotel Guest	Total	Daily Sales
Breakfast	$4.00*	100	40	140	$560
Lunch	$6.00*	25	60	85	$510
Dinner	$10.00*	50	80	130	$1,300
Total	$6.68**	175	180	355	$2,370

*Based on number of covers
**Based on total number of covers

Food for year 1995	Sales	Covers	Average Check
Dining room	$865,050	127,750	$6.68
Banquet	$334,950	47,850	$7.00
Total	$1,200,000	175,600	$6.83

7. Beverage Statistics:

	Sales	Covers	Average Cover
Dining room	$141,640	78,475*	$1.80
Banquet	$ 94,910	47,850	$1.98
Total	$236,550	126,325	$1.87
Lounge	$243,450	N/A	N/A
Total	$480,000	N/A	N/A
*Lunch and Dinner covers only			

8. Food and Beverage Department Expense:

	1993	1994	1995
China, Glass, Silver, Linen	$ 25,520	$ 27,100	$ 23,520
Contract Cleaning	5,800	6,100	7,640
Laundry	13,950	14,050	15,120
Supplies	41,280	44,700	46,300
Uniforms	4,300	4,950	5,540
Entertainment	56,900	57,300	60,200
Other Expenses	20,250	10,800	9,680
Total	$168,000	$165,000	$168,000

★ Star Motel
Comparative Balance Sheet

Assets		As of December 31	
	1993	1994	1995
Current Assets			
Cash	$600,000	$350,000	$100,000
Accounts Receivable	$730,000	$660,000	$510,000
Income Tax Receivable		$237,000	$390,000
Inventory (Food 40%, Bvg. 60%)	$180,000	$180,000	$120,000
Prepaid Insurance	$ 15,000	$ 15,000	$ 15,000
Total Current Assets	$1,525,000	$1,442,000	$1,135,000
Fixed Assets			
Land 20 Acres	$600,000	$600,000	$600,000
Building (40 Yr. S/L)	$6,600,000	$6,600,000	$6,600,000
Furn. & Equipment (10 Yr. S/L)	$900,000	$900,000	$900,000
Operating Equipment (10 Yr. S/L)	$150,000	$150,000	$150,000
Total Cost	$8,250,000	$8,250,000	$8,250,000
Less Accum. Depreciation	$810,000	$1,080,000	$1,350,000
Net Value Fixed Assets	$7,440,000	$7,170,000	$6,90,000
Other Assets			
Deferred Charges (5 yr)	$ 30,000	$ 15,000	
Deposits	$ 30,000	$ 30,000	$ 30,000
Total Other Assets	$ 60,000	$ 45,000	$ 30,000
Total Assets	$9,025,000	$8,657,000	$8,065,000
Liabilities & Stockholders Equity			
Current Liabilities			
Note Payable Demand 15%			$300,000
Accounts Payable	$219,000	$495,000	$408,000
Accrued Expenses	$ 60,000	$ 90,000	$ 60,000
Income Tax Payable	$ 88,000		
Current Portion Mortgage	$ 69,000	$ 75,000	$ 84,000
Total Current Liabilities	$436,000	$660,000	$852,000
Long Term Debt Mortgage 14% Due 2009	$6,357,000	$6,282,000	$6,198,000
Total Liabilities	$6,793,000	$6,942,000	$7,050,000
Stockholders' Equity			
Common Stock $10.00 par	$100,000	$100,000	$100,000
Capital Surplus	$900,000	$900,000	$900,000
Retained Earnings	$1,232,000	$715,000	$ 15,000
Total Stockholders' Equity	$2,232,000	$1,715,000	$1,015,000
Total Liabilities and Stockholders' Equity	$9,025,000	$8,657,000	$8,065,000

★ Star Motel
Comparative Statement of Operations
For the year ended December 31

	Amounts			Percentage to room sales		
	1993	1994	1995	1993	1994	1995
Rooms						
Sales	$2,760,000	$246,000	$180,000	100.00%	100.00%	100.00%
Departmental exp.						
Payroll & Related	$432,000	$570,600	$420,000	15.65%	23.20%	23.33%
Other	$188,400	$276,000	$210,000	6.83%	11.22%	11.67%
Total expenses	$620,400	$846,600	$630,000	22.48%	34.41%	35.00%
Dept. Income Rooms	$2,139,600	$1,613,400	$1,170,000	77.52%	65.59%	65.00%
Food and beverage sales						
Food	$1,120,000	$1,200,000	$1,120,000	71.43%	71.43%	71.43%
Beverage	$480,000	$480,000	$480,000	28.57%	28.57%	28.57%
Total sales	$1,680,000	$1,680,000	$1,680,000	100.00%	100.00%	100.00%
Cost of Sales						
Food Cost	$552,000	$833,400	$895,200	46.00%	69.45%	74.60%
Beverage Cost	$213,600	$327,600	$264,000	44.50%	68.28%	55.00%
Total cost	$765,600	$1,161,000	$1,159,200	47.57%	69.11%	69.00%
Gross profit	$914,400	$519,000	$520,800	54.43%	30.89%	31.00%
Other net income	$60,000	$45,000	$30,000	3.57%	2.68%	1.79%
Gross Profit &						
Other Income	$974,400	$564,000	$550,800	58.00%	33.57%	32.79%
Dept. Oper. Expenses						
Payroll & Related	$612,000	$695,400	$688,800	36.43%	41.39%	41.00%
Other	$168,000	$165,000	$168,000	10.00%	9.82%	10.00%
Total Dept. Expenses	$780,000	$860,400	$856,800	46.43%	51.21%	51.00%
Dept. Income F & B	$194,400	($296,400)	($306,000)	11.57%	-17.64%	-18.21%
Telephone	($30,000)	($27,000)	($24,000)	-1.09%	-1.10%	-1.33%
Minor Oper. Dept.	$30,000	$27,000	$24,000	1.09%	1.10%	1.33%
Store Rentals	$30,000	$30,000	$30,000	1.09%	1.22%	1.67%
Operated Departments						
Net Income	$2,364,000	$1,347,000	$894,000	85.65%	54.76%	49.67%

Undistributed Operating expenses				
Administrative & Gen.				
Payroll & Related	$193,200	$172,200	7.00%	7.00%
Other	$248,400	$221,400	9.00%	9.00%
Total Adm. & Gen.	$441,600	$393,600	16.00%	16.00%
Marketing	$165,600	$147,600	6.00%	6.00%
Energy	$193,200	$172,200	7.00%	7.00%
POM	$163,200	$232,200	5.91%	9.44%
Total Unds. Oper. Exp.	$963,600	$945,600	34.91%	38.44%
Net income before Fixed charges	$1,400,400	$401,400	50.74%	16.32%
Fixed charges				
Municipal taxes	$122,400	$119,400	4.43%	4.85%
Insurance	$40,000	$50,000	1.45%	2.03%
Total fixed charges	$162,400	$169,400	5.88%	6.89%
Net income before Interest & depreciation	($80,000)	$232,000	44.86%	9.43%
Interest expense	$707,000	$701,000	25.62%	28.50%
Net income before Depreciation	$531,000	($469,000)	19.24%	-19.07%
Depreciation & Amortization	$285,000	$285,000	10.33%	11.59%
Net income (loss) Before taxes	$264,000	($754,000)	8.91%	-30.65%
Provision for income Tax exp.(Refund) (2)	$880,000	($237,000)	3.19%	-9.63%
Net income (Loss)	$158,000	($517,000)	5.72%	-21.02%

Additional column (rightmost):

Payroll & Related	8.67%
Other	10.67%
Total Adm. & Gen.	19.33%
Marketing	6.30%
Energy	7.00%
POM	10.33%
Total Unds. Oper. Exp.	42.97%
Net income before Fixed charges	6.70%
Municipal taxes	6.70%
Insurance	4.44%
Total fixed charges	11.14%
Net income before Interest & depreciation	-4.44%
Interest expense	40.28%
Net income before Depreciation	-44.72%
Depreciation & Amortization	15.83%
Net income (loss) Before taxes	-60.56%
Tax exp.(Refund) (2)	-21.67%
Net income (Loss)	-38.89%

(1) Percentages are to room sales except food & beverage % are to F & B sales
(2) For illustrative purpose the refund of taxes and related account receivable is recorded. Estimates income tax at an effective rate of 40%.

Case Study

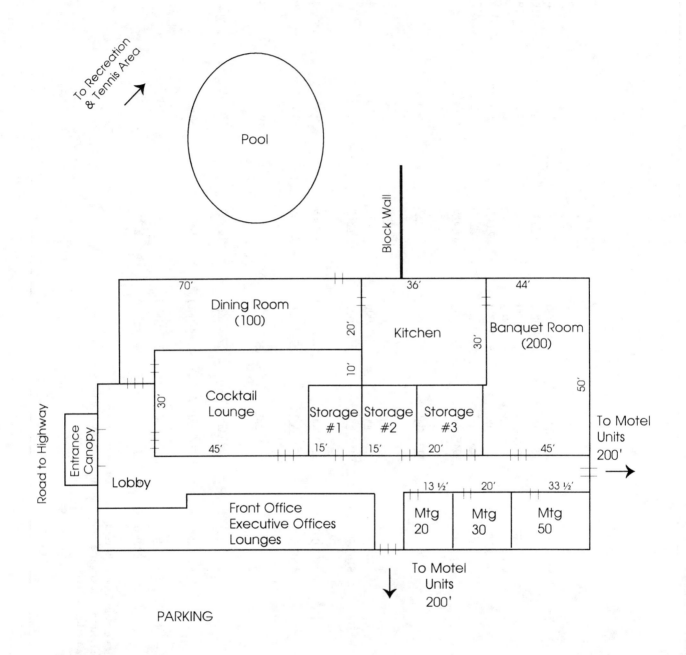

Star Motel
Commons Area
¼" = 5'

★ Phase—I

IMMEDIATE PLAN:
OPERATIONAL AND FINANCIAL

THERE ARE 14 SECTIONS TO BE COMPLETED IN SEQUENCE OR AS YOU PREFER:

Hotel Department Primarily Involved:	General Manager
Planned Completion Date:	Week I/Day 1
Instructor's Manual Reference:	Section 1
Operational and Financial Planning Guide Description:	1. Prepare a brief summary of your initial findings before any detailed and deep analysis, in other words your "Gut Reaction." Do this in outline form, probably limited to 5 to 6 items on one page.
Hotel Department Primarily Involved:	Controller prepares for General Manager
Planned Completion Date:	Week I/Day 2
Instructor's Manual Reference:	Section 2
Operational and Financial Planning Guide Description:	2. Calculate all ratios, complete financial analysis. These ratios should include **Liquidity, Solvency and Leverage and Profitability and Rate of Return Ratios.** **Activity Operating Ratios.** Analyze these financial and operating ratios for the year 1993, 1994 and 1995, comparing them to industry averages as well as to the trends established over the years within Star Motel. (Forms are at end of sections)
Hotel Department Primarily Involved:	Director of Marketing and Controller prepare for General Manager
Planned Completion Date:	Week I/Day 2
Instructor's Manual Reference:	Section 3
Operational and Financial Planning Guide Description:	3. Use all Room Demand data presented to estimate and define the total area occupancy Percentage and the total number of rooms demanded for 1995-2000 based solely, on the data presented. Discuss the reasons for any changes, both increase or decrease, from these room counts and occupancy percentages based on your management team's judgement about the quality and accuracy of the demand data presented. (Note: Normally the area demand from the hotels will differ from the area demand from government sources.)
Hotel Department Primarily Involved:	Director of Marketing, Front Office Manager, and Controller prepare for General Manager
Planned Completion Date:	Week I/Day 3
Instructor's Manual Reference:	Section 4
Operational and Financial Planning Guide Description:	4. **Evaluate Competitive Position.** Explain Star Motel's competitive position. Prepare a schedule of total rooms available and by hotel for 1993-2000. Prepare a schedule of total rooms occupied by hotel and total for 1993-1995. Prepare a schedule of total rooms occupied by hotel and total 1998-2000 assuming **even distribution** which is called the "Share of the market" approach. Finally do by hotel and in total a room demand and occupancy analysis in a chart accompanied with a written discussion based on your initial findings. (Note: In Phase II you will revise your findings based on your more thorough analysis).

Hotel Department Primarily Involved:	Director of Marketing, Controller, Front Office Manager
Planned Completion Date:	Week I/Day 4
Instructor's Manual Reference:	Section 5
Operational and Financial Planning Guide Description:	

5. Determine the 1996 Room Occupancy for Star Motel based on all the findings to date. Prepare a revised schedule of number of rooms demanded per day in the area and a distribution to both Star Motel and Bay's Inn in 1996. You must consider that the annual occupancy is over 365 days in a year which includes high, low and shoulder occupancy periods. It is suggested that you do the percentage occupancy and number of occupied rooms for the area and each hotel by day or the week as shown on the following chart.

199__ By Day of the Week Occupancy Percentage				
Day	Area Total	Star Motel	Bay's Inn	Holinite Inn
Monday				
Tuesday				
Wednesday				
Thursday				
Friday				
Saturday				
Sunday				
Average				

Duplicate the above chart for by day of the week for number of Occupied Rooms.
Use these charts for your projections of all seasons and years 1996-2000.

Hotel Department Primarily Involved:	All department heads prepare for General Manager
Planned Completion Date:	Week I/Day 5
Instructor's Manual Reference:	Section 6
Operational and Financial Planning Guide Description:	

6. **Characteristics**
Identify and list in **order of priority** the major opportunities and operating problems facing Star Motel in 1996. Prepare a numbered list of ten positive characteristics. Prepare a second numbered list of ten negative characteristics. Prepare a third numbered list of ten suggestions as to what immediate steps can be taken to improve the above named operational opportunities and

	deficiencies in 1996. Include a brief analysis of each of the 30 items.
Hotel Department Primarily Involved: Planned Completion Date: Instructor's Manual Reference: Operational and Financial Planning Guide Description:	Director of Marketing prepares for General Manager Week II/Day 1 Section 7 7. Develop a complete marketing plan. This should include: an identification of marketing mix variables which are sensitive to change; a "Major Strategy Statement"; objectives; a complete description of how best to use the area's growth factors, (e.g. R & D Center, Industrial Park, increased traffic); and any other pertinent aspects of an overall marketing strategy. Product – Promotion – Positioning – Price Determine Star Motel's competetive position. Some of the options to be considered include: A. Maintain its present profile; define it B. Low profile—compete with Bay's Inn; C. Middle profile—compete with Holinite Inn; D. High profile; or E. Combination of these approaches
Hotel Department Primarily Involved: Planned Completion Date: Instructor's Manual Reference: Operational and Financial Planning Guide Description:	General Manager with Department Heads Week II/Day 2 Section 8 8. Present in starting date order a definite timetable for implementation of all the major changes you will institute commencing February 1, 1996 and ending December 31, 1996. (Note: for the most part these are items listed in 5 and 6 above). Be specific. Where must emphasis be placed to meet realizable immediate goals? For each item explain the "Who, What, When, Where, Why" and the expected cost or savings or sales or combination.

Financial Statements

| Hotel Department Primarily Involved:

Planned Completion Date:
Instructor's Manual Reference
Operational and Financial
Planning Guide Description: | Controller with each Department Head for General Manager approval
Week II / Day 3, 4
Section 9

9. Prepare Pro-Forma Statements of Operations for 1996 compared to 1995. Use 14 column paper, headed as shown below, or 13 column paper.
Percentages are to room sales except that food and beverage percentages are to food and beverage sales. For each and every line item on your Pro-Forma Statements of Operations present in writing how you obtained your amounts for 1996 from those reported in 1995, 1994, and 1993. A supplementary schedule should be written to support each calculation with proper cross-indexing. |

12   Case Study

Column Numbers									
1, 2, 3,	4	5	6	7	8	9	10	11,12,13,14	
	Amounts			Percentages				
Item	1996	1995	Diff	1996	1995	Diff	Support Schedule Number	Comments

Hotel Department Primarily Involved: Controller for General Manager
Planned Completion Date: Week II/Day 3, 4
Instructor's Manual Reference: Section 10
Operational and Financial
Planning Guide Description.

10. Prepare a Pro-Forma Balance Sheet, "Pro-Forma Statement of Cash Receipts and and Disbursements" and "Pro-Forma Statement of Quick Cash Flow" for the year ending December 31, 1996. Briefly discuss any significant differences relating the **Pro-Forma Balance Sheet** to the **Pro-Forma Statement of Cash Receipts and Disbursements and Pro-Forma Statement of Quick Cash Flow**, on supplemental supportive schedules properly referenced to the Statement.

Cash Flow Projection	
	Year
Estimated "Cash Inflow" from Operations	
Net Income–After Tax	xxx
Add Back: Depreciation & Amortization	xxx
Total from Operations	xxx
Add New Financing & Other Loans	xxx
Total Cash Inflow	**xxx**
Less: Cash Outflow	
Principal Payments on Debt	xxx
Capital Improvements Paid in Cash	xxx
Dividends	xxx
Other	xxx
Total Cash Outflow	**xxx**
"Cash Flow" excess or (deficiency)	**xxx**

Hotel Department Primarily Involved: Controller for General Manager
Planned Completion Date: Week II/Day 3, 4
Instructor's Manual Reference: Section 11
Operational and Financial
Planning Guide Description:

11. Prepare a **Pro-Forma Statement of Cash Receipts and Cash Disbursements by month and for the year ending December, 1996**. Prepare by **month** and the **total** for the year on 13 column paper with item space. This will indicate cash needs and or cash for savings accounts on a monthly basis.

Hotel Department Primarily Involved:	Controller for General Manager approval
Planned Completion Date:	Week II/Day 3, 4
Instructor's Manual Reference:	Section 12
Operational and Financial Planning Guide Description:	12. Prepare a **Pro-Forma Statement of "Cash Flow" for the years ending December 31, 1996, 1997, 1998, 1999 and 2000.**

Cash Flow Projection	Year
Estimated "Cash Inflow" from Operations	
Net Income–After Tax	xxx
Add Back: Depreciation & Amortization	<u>xxx</u>
Total from Operations	xxx
Add New Financing & Other Loans	<u>xxx</u>
Total Cash Inflow	<u>xxx</u>
Less: Cash Outflow	
Principal Payments on Debt	xxx
Capital Improvements Paid in Cash	xxx
Dividends	xxx
Other	<u>xxx</u>
Total Cash Outflow	<u>xxx</u>
"Cash Flow" excess or (deficiency)	<u>xxx</u>

Hotel Department Primarily Involved:	General Manager and Controller with each Department Head
Planned Completion Date:	Week III/Day 1, 2
Instructor's Manual Reference:	Section 13
Operational and Financial Planning Guide Description:	13. Prepare a written analysis of the Pro-Forma Statements. Indicate the high and low points of the Company's operating and financial position during and at the end of the year. Include your explanation of how it is better off and/or worse off than at present.
Hotel Department Primarily Involved:	Executive Department Heads with Controller and then with General Manager
Planned Completion Date	Week III Day 2
Instructor's Manual Reference:	Section 14
Operational and Financial Planning Guide Description:	14. **Capital Expenditures** Determine a capital improvement (expenditure) program from 1996-2000. Prepare a meeting room demand by size by year and resulting conclusions. Prepare a room demand by year by hotel with Star Motel concentrating on the meeting business. Optional to the case is to do the following: Calculate the net present value of additional marginal profits brought about by the capital improvement programs. Calculate the net present value of lost marginal profit if the various programs are not implemented. Draw conclusions. Present your total program in understandable format. Develop an implementation plan.

Hotel Department Primarily Involved:	Executive Department Heads with Controller and then with General Manager
Planned Completion Date	Week III Day 3
Instructor's Manual Reference:	Section 15
Operational and Financial Planning Guide Description:	15. Pro-Forma Comparative Statements of Operations. a. Sales, Expenses and Profit Forecast Project sales, expenses profit for 1996, 1997, 1998, 2000. The projection should be in the format of the attached statements for 1995, 1994, and 1993. Do the 5 years for amounts and percentages on one page. The basis of the Room Sales Projection is the number of room nights demanded. At this time you must return to Phase 1, Item 4 "Evaluate Competitive Position" and prepare a final revised occupancy analysis. Do not forget that it must include all of Phase I plus the results of the Capital Improvement Program in Phase II.
Hotel Department Primarily Involved:	General Manager
Planned Completion Date:	Week III/Day 3, 4
Instructor's Manual Reference:	Section 16
Operational and Financial Planning Guide Description:	16. **Conclusion** The **Final Step** is to prepare a summary and conclusions which is generally limited to one to three pages, and is a part of the opening letter in the report. Note: It is what the Board of Directors will read and use to judge you and your performance.
Hotel Department Primarily Involved:	General Manager with Chief Engineer then Department Heads
Instructor's Manual Reference:	Optional
Operational and Financial Planning Guide Description	**Floor Plan** Based upon your consulting team's conclusions, draw a new floor plan for Star Motel including any additions, alterations, or improvements with measurement to scale. The present floor plan is attached.

★ Property Analysis

Ratio to Total Revenue (Sales)

This worksheet will provide a quick analysis of how your property is performing in comparison to the industry.

	Your property	Comparison 1	Comparison 2	Comparison 3	Comparison 4	Comparison 5
Revenues						
Rooms		60.0%	62.0%	63.5%	59.0%	
Food		24.0	25.5	23.0	26.0	
Beverage		10.0	8.7	11.00	10.0	
Other Food and Beverage		1.4	1.1	1.5	1.4	
Telephone		2.4	2.2	2.3	2.3	
Minor-Operated		1.0	2.1	1.2	1.0	
Rentals & Other		1.2	1.6	0.8	1.1	
Total Revenue		100.0	100.0	100.0	100.0	
Department Expense						
Rooms		16.0	17.0	15.8	14.4	
Food & Beverage		29.0	32.5	28.7	30.4	
Telephone		2.0	2.1	2.4	2.3	
Minor-Operated		0.8	1.9	0.6	1.3	
Total Operated Dept. Expense		47.0	49.0	42.8	46.0	
Department Profit						
Rooms		45.0	45.1	49.0	43.2	
Food & Beverage		6.0	3.8	7.5	7.3	
Telephone		.4	0.1	<0.2>	0.1	
Minor-Operated		.2	.4	0.6	0.1	
Rentals & Other		.2	1.7	0.7	1.0	
Total Operated Dept. Profit		54.0	51.8	58.0	54.0	
Undistributed Expenses						
Administrative & General						
Payroll & Related		4.7	5.6	4.6	4.5	
Other		5.7	6.3	5.8	5.5	
Total		10.6	11.8	9.5	9.8	
Marketing						
Payroll & Related		2.0	2.1	1.9	1.9	
Other		5.0	3.8	4.6	4.6	
Total		7.0	5.8	5.9	6.3	
Energy		5.8	5.7	5.8	5.6	
Property Operation & Maintenance		5.1	5.3	5.2	5.2	
Total Undistributed Expenses		28.3	29.5	27.3	26.7	
Income Before Mngt. Fees & Fixed Chgs.		25.0	24.0	29.5	26.9	
Management Fees (Base & Incentive)		3.5	3.5	3.4	3.4	
Income Before Fixed Charges		22.8	22.0	26.9	25.4	
Fixed Charges		28.0	27.5	32.2	30.0	
Income Before Income Taxes		3.0%	<3.2>%	<4.6>%	<3.0>%	
Reserve for Capital Replacement		2.1%	2.6%	2.0%	1.7%	

Amounts and Percentages will not add due to the use of industry numbers reported by line by hotels.

★ Property Analysis

Ratio to Total Revenue (Sales)

This worksheet will provide a quick analysis of how your property is performing in comparison to the industry.

	Your property	Comparison 1	Comparison 2	Comparison 3	Comparison 4	Comparison 5
Revenues						
Rooms						
Food						
Beverage						
Other Food and Beverage						
Telephone						
Minor-Operated						
Rentals & Other						
Total Revenue						
Operated Department Expense						
Rooms						
Food & Beverage						
Telephone						
Minor-Operated						
Total Operated Dept. Expense						
Operated Department Profit						
Rooms						
Food & Beverage						
Telephone						
Minor-Operated						
Rentals & Other						
Total Operated Dept. Profit						
Undistributed Expenses						
Administrative & General						
Payroll & Related						
Other						
Total						
Marketing						
Payroll & Related						
Other						
Total						
Energy						
Property Operation & Maintenance						
Total Undistributed Expenses						
Income Before Mngt. Fees & Fixed Chgs.						
Management Fees (Base & Incentive)						
Income Before Fixed Charges						
Fixed Charges						
Income Before Income Taxes						
Reserve for Capital Replacement						

Liquidity Ratios

Ratio Name Formula	Computation	Results	Comparative Guide	Analysis & Interpretation
1. **Current Ratio** Current Assets / Current Liabilities				
2. **Quick Ratio** Cash and Marketable Securities / Accounts Receivable Current Liabilities				
3. **Account Rec. %** Avg. Acct. Rec. / Total Revenues				
4. **Acct. Rec. Turnover** Total Revenues / Avg. Acct. Rec. Or 1 / Acct. Rec. %				
5. **Number of Days Sales Uncollected** 365 / Acc. Rec. Turnover Or Avg. Acct. Rec. / One Days Sales				

Solvency and Leverage Ratios

Ratio Name Formula	Computation	Results	Comparative Guide	Analysis & Interpretation
1. Solvency Ratio Total Assets Total Liabilities				
2. Debt to Total Asset Ratio Total Liabilities Total Assets or 1 Solvency Ratio				
3. Debt to Equity Ratio Total Liabilities Total Stockholders Equity				
4. Number of Times Interest Earned Net Profit Before Tax & Interest Interest				

Profitability and Rate of Return Ratios

Ratio Name Formula	Computation	Results	Comparative Guide	Analysis & Interpretation
1. **Fixed Assets Turnover** $\dfrac{\text{Total Revenues}}{\text{Avg. Total Fix Assets}}$				
2. **Return on Owners Equity** $\dfrac{\text{Net Profit After Tax}}{\text{Avg. Stockholder Equity}}$				
3. **Return on Assets** $\dfrac{\text{Net Profit Before Tax \& Interest}}{\text{Avg Total Assets}}$				
4. **Net Return on Assets** $\dfrac{\text{Net Profit After Tax}}{\text{Avg Total Assets}}$				
5. **Profit Margin** $\dfrac{\text{Net Profit After Tax}}{\text{Total Revenues}}$				
6. **Operating Efficiency Ratio** $\dfrac{\text{Income Before Fix Chg}}{\text{Total Revenues}}$				
7. **Total Assets Turnover** $\dfrac{\text{Net Sales}}{\text{Total Assets}}$				

Profitability and Rate of Return Ratios

Ratio Name Formula	Computation	Results	Comparative Guide	Analysis & Interpretation
8. Du Pont Analysis Return on Assets Net Profit Margin X Total Assets Turnover				

Activity Operating Ratios

Ratio Name Formula	Computation	Results	Comparative Guide	Analysis & Interpretation
1. **Food Inventory Turnover** $\dfrac{\text{Cost of Food Sold}}{\text{Avg. Food Inventory}}$				
2. **No. of Days Food on Hand** $\dfrac{365}{\text{Food Inventory}}$				
3. **Food Cost %** $\dfrac{\text{Cost of Food Sold}}{\text{Food Sales}}$				
4. **Avg. Food Sales Per Cover** $\dfrac{\text{Food Sales}}{\text{No. Cover Served}}$	Given In Case			
5. **Bev. Inv. Turnover** $\dfrac{\text{Cost of Bev. Sold}}{\text{Avg. Bev. Inv.}}$				
6. **No. Days Bev. on Hand** $\dfrac{365}{\text{Bev. Inv. Turnover}}$				
7. **Avg. Bev. Sales Cover** $\dfrac{\text{Bev. Sales/}}{\text{No. Cover Served}}$	Given In Case			

Activity Operating Ratios

Ratio Name Formula	Computation	Results	Comparative Guide	Analysis & Interpretation
8. **Bev. Cost Percentage** Cost of Bev. Sold / Beverage Sales				
9. **Occupancy %** Rooms Sold / Rms Available for Sale				
10. **Multiple (Double) Occupancy %** No. Of Guests / Rms Sold or Excess of Guests Over Rms Sold / Rooms Sold				
11. **Avg. Room Rate** Rms Sales / Rms Sold				
12. **Avg. Guest Rate** Rms Sales / No. Of Guests				
13. **Avg. Rms. Sales Per Available Room Per Day** Rooms Sales Per Day / No. Rms Avail. Daily				

Section 1:

Summary of Initial Findings

★ Instruction

Purpose:

To get a feeling for the Motel's performances. Is it good, bad, average? Also to get a feeling for the environment in which it operates.

How to Achieve this Goal:

- → Have a pad of paper, pencils and a post it pad with you as you conduct your evaluation.
- → Read the entire study thoroughly.
- → Write down your "gut reactions".
- → Write down what seems abnormal, positive, negative and all your comments. For example, percentages of occupancy (are they increasing or decreasing?), revenue (increasing or decreasing?), etc...
- → Find out about the area in which the Motel operates: is there an increasing or decreasing demand; how is the competition doing compared to the Star Motel?
- → Draw some preliminary conclusions: where does the Motel stand; what seems to be the problems; what are our strengths and weaknesses; what are the opportunities?

★ Solution

Our initial comments based on all the available information of area demand, (present and projected), and the present limitations of Star Motel to meet those demands, and also, after reviewing the financial reports for the last three years, and the costs of future capital improvements necessary to attract a greater volume of business, are as follows:

The occupancy rate has declined from a high of 90% to a low of 60%. This is, in part, due to increased competition from Bay's Inn; resulting from the absence of or the inadequate marketing plan of the Star Motel. Star Motel has the advantage over Bay's Inn, to offer better services and facilities, and a strong and accurate marketing plan is needed to accentuate those services offered by Star Motel and not available in the competition.

The local market shows signs of substantial growth in the coming years, especially in the area of business meetings. Star Motel appears to be in a position to meet these demands by slightly converting or modifying its facilities.

Food and beverage sales have remained constant, while costs and expenses have risen substantially and in disproportion, indicating a lack of control over these costs, and a lack of imagination in order to increase revenue in this department. In the Food and Beverage area, new plans, new methods of control, and new procedures must be established, implemented, and adhered to.

Finally, it is our opinion that while certain capital improvements may be necessary in the near future in order to meet a potential demand, Star Motel's biggest problem is an operational problem. A detailed study should reveal precisely the amount of business that the motel should realize. This amount should be set as a goal for the present management team in each department to achieve; otherwise there will be no other alternative, except to bring in a new team.

Section 2:

Ratio Analysis

28 SECTION 2

★ Instruction

Purpose:
Ratio analysis will permit us to examine and evaluate the firm's financial position regarding liquidity, solvency, leverage, profitability, and the operational performances during the last three years, as well as detecting trends.

How to achieve that purpose:
→ Balance sheets for the last three years are needed.
→ Statements of operations for the last three years are also needed.

After computing these ratios, the figures will be compared to the industry averages, to determine where our company stands in relation to the industry in general. Once this is done, analyzing this ratio would be a matter of comparing these computed numbers to determine performances over the years by comparing the results to the industry averages. Trends will be determined by comparing a year's results to the previous year's.

These ratios must be broken into four separate groups:

A. Liquidity Ratios.
B. Solvency and Leverage Ratios.
C. Profitability and Rate of Return Ratios.
D. Activity and Operating Ratios.

★ Solution

A. Liquidity Ratios
Purpose: To evaluate the Motel's ability to meet short-term obligations. These figures are of interest to short-term creditors and management.
How to achieve that purpose:
This evaluation has to take into consideration the results of five ratios.

1. **Current Ratio**—used as first indicator to measure the ability to meet short-term obligations. It is computed as follows:

$$\text{Current ratio} = \frac{\text{Current Assets}}{\text{Current Liabilities}}$$

These figures are found in the balance sheet. For example, the current ratio for 1995 is computed by dividing $1,135,000 by $852,000. The result is 1.35. It is expressed in this manner: 1.35 to 1, or 1.35:1. This means that every dollar in current debt is covered by $1.35 in current assets.

2. **Quick Ratio**—serves the same purpose as the current ratio, however as a conservative measure, inventories and prepaids are excluded from current assets. The reason for this is because a sale has to be made to get cash or they are not always that easy to turn into cash. It is computed as follows:

$$\text{Quick Ratio} = \frac{\text{Current Assets - Inventories and Prepds.}}{\text{Current Liabilities}}$$

These figures are found on the balance sheets. For example, the quick ratio for 1995 would be computed by subtracting $120,000 for inventories and $15,000 for prepaid insurance from $1,135,000 which is the total current assets, and then the answer is divided by $852,000 of total current liabilities, resulting in 1.17. It is expressed in the same manner as the current ratio, 1.17:1. This figure will be compared to the industry average to determine where our company stands in relation to the industry in general. The higher this ratio, as compared to the industry average, the better the company's liquid position.

3. **Accounts Receivable**—indicates percent of total annual sales that were credit sales. It is computed as follows:

$$\text{Accounts Receivable Percentage} \frac{\text{Average Acc. Rec.}}{} = \text{Total Revenue}$$

These figures are found on the balance sheets and income statements. For example, the accounts receivable percentage is computed by dividing $510,000 (balance sheet) by $3,540,000 (total revenue from income statement), which is approximately 15%. (Total revenue equals rooms $1,800,000 plus food and beverage $1,680,000 plus F & B other income $30,000, plus telephone <loss> <$24,000>, plus minor operated depts $24,000, plus store rentals $30,000 totals $3,540,000). The lower this ratio, compared to the industry average, the more liquid the company is.

4. **Accounts Receivable Turnover (T/O)**—the primary purpose is to provide a denominator in the average collection period calculation. It is computed as follows:

$$\text{Accounts Receivable T/O} = \frac{\text{Total Revenue}}{\text{Average Accounts Receivable}}$$

These figures are found on the income statement and the balance sheet. For example, in 1995, the accounts receivable T/O is calculated by dividing $3,540,000 (income statement) by $510,000 (balance sheet) which equals 6.9 times. The higher this ratio, compared to the industry average, the more liquid the company is.

5. **Number of Days Sales Uncollected**—this ratio indicates the efficiency of the firm's collection and credit policies and procedures. The number of days that have elapsed between the sale and the collection. It is calculated as follows:

$$\text{Number of Days Uncoll.} = \frac{365}{\text{Accounts Receivable T/O}}$$

This figure is found by taking 365 days divided by the accounts receivable T/O found in #4 of liquidity ratios. For example, in 1995, 365 was divided by 6.9 which equals 53 days. The fewer the days, as compared to the industry average, the better the company's liquidity.

	Liquidity Ratios			
	1993	1994	1995	Industry Average
Current Ratio	3.50:1	2.18:1	1.33:1	1:1
Quick Ratio	3.05:1	1.89:1	1.17:1	.80:1
Accounts Receivable %	16%	16%	15%	3.7%
Accounts Receivable T/O	6.2x	6.3x	6.9x	15-30x
Number of Days Sales Uncollected	59	58	53	12-24 Days

Liquidity ratios indicate a firm's ability to meet short-term obligations. They are of big interest to short-term creditors.

It is true that Star Motel has an above average current and quick ratios, but the speed at which they are falling is a source of discomfort to the reader, especially at a time when no expansion nor any other investment activity is occurring.

The ratios related to accounts receivable show that a high percent of sales were credit sales. These credit sales are collected over long periods of time as compared to the industry average. Star Motel's policies and procedures related to credit collection are inefficient and must be reviewed.

The income tax receivable is the result of the carry-back to a taxable year the net operating loss of a current year. It is excluded from the accounts receivable discussion since it is not the result of a sale to a customer.

B. **Solvency and Leverage Ratios**
Purpose: To evaluate the Motel's ability to honor long-term obligations. These ratios are of interest to management, long term creditors, and sometimes, potential investors.
How to achieve that purpose:
This evaluation has to take into consideration the results of the four following ratios:

1. **Solvency Ratio**—indicated dollars in assets available to cover each dollar in liabilities. It is computed as follows:

$$\text{Solvency Ratio} = \frac{\text{Total Assets}}{\text{Total Liabilities}}$$

   These figures are found in the balance sheets. For example, the solvency ratio for 1995 is computed by dividing $8,065,000, of total assets by $7,050,000 of total liabilities, resulting in 1.14. It would be expressed in this manner, 1.14:1, which means that every dollar in total liabilities is covered by $1.14 in total assets. The higher this ratio, as compared to the industry average, the more solvent the Motel is.

2. **Debt Ratio**—indicates the percentage of assets that are financed by debt. It is also an indicator of leverage. It is computed as follows:

$$\text{Debt Ratio} = \frac{\text{Total Liabilities}}{\text{Total Assets}}$$

$$\text{or} \quad \frac{1}{\text{Solvency Ratio}}$$

   These figures are found in the balance sheets. For example, the debt ratio for 1995, is computed by dividing $7,050,000 of total liabilities, by $8,065,000 of total assets, or dividing 1 by 1.14 of solvency ratio. The debt ratio will be .87 or 87% in both cases. The lower the percentage of this ratio, the better the Motel's long-term debt position is.

3. **Debt to Equity Ratio**—indicates that for every dollar invested by stockholders the dollars provided for debt. It is computed as follows:

$$\text{Debt to Equity Ratio} = \frac{\text{Total Liabilities}}{\text{Total Stockholders' Equity}}$$

   These figures are found in the balance sheets. For example, the debt to equity ratio for 1995 is found by dividing $7,050,000 of total liabilities by $1,015,000 of stockholders' equity to find a debt to equity ratio of 6.95.
   It will be expressed as 6.95:1, and means that every dollar financed by stockholders, $6.95 is financed by debt.
   The lower this ratio, as compared to the industry average, the better the Motel's long-term debt position is. The higher this ratio, the greater the risk is to long-term investors and the higher leverage.

4. **Number of Times Interest Earned**—indicates the Motel's ability to make interest payments on long-term debts. It is computed as follows:

$$\text{Number of Times Int. Earned} = \frac{\text{Net Income Before Tax plus Interest}}{\text{Interest}}$$

   These figures are found in the income statements. For example, the number of times interest earned for 1993 is found by dividing $953,000 ($246,000 of net income before tax plus $707,000 interest) by $707,000 of interest, to find a number times interest earned of 1.35 times.
   The higher this ratio, as compared to the industry average, the better the Motel's long-term debt paying ability is. The lower this ratio, the higher the risk is for long-term lenders.

Solvency and Leverage Ratios				
	1993	1994	1995	Industry Average
Solvency Ratio	1.33:1	1.25:1	1.14:1	1.50:1
Debt Ratio	77%	80%	87%	67%
Debt/Equity Ratio	3.04:1	4.05:1	6.90:1	2:1
Number of Times Interest Earned	1.35x	negative	negative	5x

Solvency and leverage ratios indicate a firm's ability to meet long-term debt obligations. These ratios are of interest to long-term creditors and potential investors.

Star Motel's solvency ratios show that the motel is more highly leveraged as compared to the industry average: If this ratio continues to decrease, future borrowing may be more difficult.

The level of leverage at the Star Motel is higher than the industry average and is increasing as the debt ratio shows. The percentage of assets that are financed by debt, tends to be increasing. As shown in the debt/equity ratio, we can see the highly increasing leverage resulting from financing by debt as compared to financing by stockholders.

The number of times interest earned shows the ability to make interest payments on long-term debt. In our case, Star Motel is not able to generate enough revenue in order to cover its interest payments, which means that the Motel will have an increasingly hard time meeting its long-term principal payments.

Finally, none of these ratios is satisfactory, and Star Motel seems to be in a very bad long-term debt position. This will make it difficult to find new long-term debt creditors, if needed, resulting from the great risk these creditors might face.

C. **Profitability and Rate of Returns Ratios**

Purpose: To evaluate management effectiveness in generating profits from investments. These ratios are of interest to management, investors and creditors.

How to achieve that purpose:

This evaluation has to take into consideration the results of the following ratios:

1. **Fixed Assets Turnover**—indicates management effectiveness of the use of assets in generating sales. It is computes as follows:

$$\text{Fixed Assets T/O} = \frac{\text{Total Revenue}}{\text{Average Fixed Assets (at net value)*}}$$

These figures are found both in the balance sheets (fixed assets) and the income statement (total revenue).

For example, the fixed assets T/O for 1995 is computed by dividing $3,540,000 of total revenue by $6,900,000 of fixed assets to find a fixed assets turnover of .51 times per year.

The higher this ratio, as compared to the industry average, the better is the use of fixed assets in generating sales.

2. **Return on Owners' Equity**—indicates management effectiveness in the use of owners' equity in generating sales. It is computed as follows:

$$\text{Return on Equity} = \frac{\text{Net Profit after Tax}}{\text{Average Stockholders' Equity*}}$$

These figures are found in both the balance sheet (stockholders' equity) and the income statement (net profit after tax).

For example, the return on owners' equity in 1993 is determined by dividing $158,000 of net profit after tax, by $2,232,000 of stockholders' equity. The result is .07 or 7%. This means the rate of return on owners' equity was 7%. The higher this percentage, the better the rate of return on owners' equity.

3. **Return on Assets**—measures management effectiveness in the use of all assets. If compared to the interest rate, it could be a good indicator in determining if debt financing is plausible. Debt financing is generally plausible only if the return on assets is greater than interest rate. This ratio is computed as follows:

$$\text{Return on Assets} = \frac{\text{Net Profit Before Tax \& Interest}}{\text{Average Total Assets*}}$$

These figures are found both on the balance sheets (total assets) and the income statements (net profit before tax and interest).
For example, in 1993, net profit before tax and interest was $953,000 divided by $9,025,000 of total assets and the result is approximately .11 or 11% return on assets. The higher this percentage for a given year, the better the rate of return on total assets.

4. **Net Return on Assets**—measures management effectiveness in the use of the Motel's assets. It is computed as follows:

$$\text{Net Return on Assets} = \frac{\text{Net Profit After Tax}}{\text{Average Total Assets*}}$$

These figures are found both in the balance sheet (total assets) and the income statement (net profit after tax). For example, in 1993, net profit after tax was $158,000 divided by $9,025,000 of total assets, resulting in .018 or 1.8% of net return on assets. The higher this percentage, as compared to the industry average, the better the rate of net return on assets.

5. **Profit Margin**—indicates the percentage of each sales dollar that results in net profit. It is not a good indicator of profitability because it does not consider investments. It is computed as follows:

$$\text{Profit Margin} = \frac{\text{Net Profit after Tax}}{\text{Total Revenue}}$$

These figures are found on the income statements. For example, in 1993, net profit after tax was $158,000 divided by $4,530,000 of total revenue. The result is .035 or 3.5% of profit margin. This means that in every dollar of sales there was 3.5 cents net profit.
The higher the percentage, the better the net profit.

6. **Operating Efficiency Ratio**—provides an indication of management in managing operation and generating profit regardless of the type of financing. It is computed as follows.

$$\text{Operating Efficiency Ratio} = \frac{\text{Income before Fixed Chg.}}{\text{Total Revenue}}$$

These figures are found on the income statements. For example, in 1993, income before fixed charges was $1,400,400 divided by $4,530,000 of total revenue, resulting in .309 or 30.9% of operating efficiency ratio.
The higher this percentage, the better and more efficient the management of the operations.

7. **Total Assets Turnover**—another method of measuring management effectiveness in utilizing the Motel's assets. It is computed as follows:

$$\text{Total Assets T/O} = \frac{\text{Net Sales}}{\text{Average Total Assets*}}$$

These figures are found both on the balance sheets (total assets) and the income statements (sales). For example, in 1993, net sales were $4,530,000 divided by total assets of $9,025,000; the result is .50 of total assets turnover.
The higher this turnover, the better is the use of the assets.

8. **DuPont Analysis: Net Return on Assets**—used to explain variations in net return on assets from year to year. Its components are profit margin; which ignores the use of assets, and total assets turnover, which ignores profitability. By bringing them together, judgement can be accurately made based on the use of assets recognized in the total assets turnover and profitability recognized by the profit margin. These figures are found in the ratio analysis. This ratio is computed as follows:

Net Return on Assets = Profit Margin X Total Asset Turnover

The analysis of these figures, will show what causes the net return on assets to increase or decrease. This question of exactly which element caused that increase or decrease will be answered. Is it because of lower or higher profitability, or lower or higher assets turnover? (There are charts which present the components of the DuPont Formula Analysis in a snapshot presentation which you are referred to if you desire further in depth study.)

Profitability and Rate of Return Ratios				
	1993	**1994**	**1995**	**Industry Average**
Fixed Assets T/O	.61	.59	.51	.85 Times/Year
Return on Owner's Equity	7%	Negative	Negative	N/A
Return on Assets	11%	Negative	Negative	5% to 12%
Net Return on Assets	1.8%	Negative	Negative	N/A
Profit Margin	3.5%	Negative	Negative	1% to 4%
Operating Efficiency Ratios	30.9%	9.5%	3.4%	22% to 34%
Total Assets T/O	.50	.49	.50	.60 to .80 Times/Year

Du Pont Analysis						
	Return on Assets	=	Profit Margin	x	Total Asset T/O	
1995	Negative	=	Negative	x	.44	
1994	Negative	=	Negative	x	.49	
1993	1.8%	=	3.5%	x	.50	

Profitability and rate of return ratios indicate management effectiveness in generating profits from investments.

In our case, Star Motel's management is not effective in the use of assets generating revenues, and not effective in utilizing equity funds. The percentage of sales dollars that results in profit in the profit margin ratio is negative. The operating efficiency ratio shows a dramatic decrease in 1994 and 1995 indicating the management ineffectiveness in profitability managing operations. Finally, the Du Pont analysis shows negative results in 1994 and 1995, due to a decrease in total asset turnover and negative amounts in the profit margin ratio.

These ratios reflect Star Motel's current unprofitable situation. In the past three years, these ratios have declined to completely unacceptable levels.

*1992 Figures are not available, therefore, averages will not be computed.

D. **Activity and Operating Ratios**
   Purpose: These ratios are used to measure the performance of the operations and management.
   How to achieve that purpose:
   In order to achieve this purpose, the following ratios must be analyzed:

   1. **Food Inventory Turnover**—This measures the efficiency of the utilization of the food inventory on hand. Each operation should develop its approximate T/O, preferably by food category, and monitor deviations. The computation is as follows:

$$\text{Food Inventory T/O} = \frac{\text{Cost of Food Sold}}{\text{Average Food Inventory}}$$

These figures are found on both the income statement and the balance sheet. For example, in 1995, when dividing $895,200, cost of food sold (income statement) by $60,000, average food inventory (Balance Sheet), the result is 14.92 times per year. The higher this ratio, the better.

2. **Number of Days Food on Hand**—This ratio also expresses the utilization of the food inventory on hand. It is expressed in number of days. It is calculated as follows:

$$\text{Number of Days Food on Hand} = \frac{365}{\text{Food Inventory T/O}}$$

For 1995, this figure is found by taking 365 days and dividing it by the food inventory turnover (14.92), resulting in 24.46 days food on hand. The lower this ratio, the better.

3. **Food Cost Percentage**—the percent of food sales required to cover food cost. This ratio is computed as follows:

$$\text{Food Cost Percentage} = \frac{\text{Cost of Food Sold}}{\text{Food Sales}}$$

These figures are found on the income statement. For example, in 1995, when we divide $895,200 by $1,200,000, the result is 75%. The lower this figure, the better.

4. **Beverage Inventory Turnover**—See Food Inventory Turnover (#1). The calculation is as follows:

$$\text{Beverage Inventory T/O} = \frac{\text{Cost of Beverage Sold}}{\text{Average Beverage Inventory}}$$

5. **Number of Days Beverages on Hand**—See Number of Days Food on Hand (#2). The calculation is as follows:

$$\text{Number of Days Bev. on Hand} = \frac{365}{\text{Beverage Inventory T/O}}$$

6. **Beverage Cost Percentage**—See Food Cost Percentage (#3). The calculation is as follows:

$$\text{Beverage Cost Percentage} = \frac{\text{Cost of Beverage Sold}}{\text{Beverage Sales}}$$

Activity and Operating Ratios Food and Beverage				
	1993	1994	1995	Industry Average
Food Inventory - T/O	7.67x	11.58x	14.92x	26x to 36x
# of Days Food on Hand	47.65	31.52	24.46	10 to 14 days
Food Cost Percentage	46%	69%	75%	32.40%
Beverage Inventory T/O	1.98x	3.03x	2.93x	6x to 9x
# of Days Beverage on Hand	194.34	120.46	124.57	40 to 60 days
Beverage Cost Percentage	45%	68%	55%	21.23%

Due to higher food costs in the past three years and to a lower food inventory in 1995, the food inventory turnover has increased, but is still far below the industry average. The food cost percentage increased from a highly unacceptable level in 1993 to an astonishing high food cost in 1995.

The beverage inventory turnover, is far behind the industry average. The beverage cost percentage was more than twice the industry average in 1993, more than three times the average in 1994, and in 1995 was at 250% above the industry.

The food and beverage turnovers and cost percentages are signs of misuse of working capital, and require investigation into waste, theft and mismanagement.

7. **Occupancy Percent**—This ratio measures the marketing success of the sales department. This ratio is calculated as follows:

$$\text{Occupancy Percent} = \frac{\text{Rooms Sold}}{\text{Rooms Available for Sale}}$$

This information is found from internal records of operation. For Star Motel, these figures were given for 1993-1995.

8. **Double Occupancy Percent**—This ratio relates to the number of guests per number of rooms occupied. The ratio is calculated as follows:

$$\text{Double Occupancy \%} = \frac{\text{Number of Guests}}{\text{Rooms Sold}}$$

These figures are also found internally. For Star Motel, these figures were given for 1993-1995. **Multiple Occupancy Percent** is the number of rooms with more than one guest and should not be confused with the double occupancy percent.

9. **Average Room Rate**—This figure is influenced by selling higher priced rooms, percent of occupancy, double occupancy and inflation. These figures are found from internal sources of operations and the income statement. For Star Motel, these figures were given for 1993-1995. The ratio is calculated as follows:

$$\text{Average Room Rate} = \frac{\text{Room Sales}}{\text{Rooms Sold}}$$

10. **Average Guest Rate**—This ratio is another way of looking at the effect of double occupancy. It is calculated as follows:

$$\text{Average Guest Rate} = \frac{\text{Room Sales}}{\text{Number of Guests}}$$

These figures are found on the income statement and internally from operations. For example, in 1995 room sales was $1,800,000 divided by 61,320 guests for the year. This results in an average guest rate of approximately $30.

11. **Average Room Sales per Available Room**—This ratio is used to observe trends, as well as for comparisons with similar hotel operations. It is calculated as follows:

$$\text{Average Room Sales per Available Room} = \frac{\text{Room Sales}}{\text{Number of Rooms Available}}$$

These figures are found on the income statements and the data given about the Motel.
For example, in 1995, room sales were $1,800,000 divided by 73,000 rooms available, resulting in an average daily room sales per available room of $25.20. You should be aware, this ratio is expressed both per day and per year.

	Activity and Operating Ratios Rooms			
	1993	1994	1995	Industry Average
Occupancy %	90%	75%	60%	65.5%
Double Occupancy %	40%	40%	40%	40.3%
Average Room Rate	42.00	45.00	42.00	53.80
Average Guest Rate	30.00	32.14	30.00	42.38
Average Room Sales per Available Room	37.80	33.75	25.20	39.00

These ratios are used to measure performance of operation in the rooms department. As we see, a steady decline in the overall occupancy percentage over the last three years is one of the major reasons for the declining (bad) financial position in which the Star Motel is now operating.

★ Summary Analysis of All the Ratios

★ Instruction

Purpose:
Summarize all ratios, by groups, on one page, in order to easily refer to them when necessary.

How to achieve this purpose:
- → Report, from previous analysis, headlines regarding each group of ratios and briefly describe what immediate steps should be taken in order to bring them back to normal.
- → These steps must be incorporated into the immediate action plan for 1996, described in a later section.
- → Base your results on performances as related to the industry averages, and on trends related to changes from year to year for each of the ratios.

★ Solution

The immediate plan of action that will be designed and implemented in 1996 will deal primarily with these operational problems detected by the analysis of all the ratios, as follows:

1. Liquidity ratios will not be permitted to fall down any further. They must be stabilized. New and effective collection policies must be implemented.
2. The motel needs to have creditors' and investors' confidence back in order to finance any future improvements. To do this, solvency and leverage ratios should be stabilized in the short-run, and through better generation of revenue in 1996 and cost control, the times interest earned ratio must improve.
3. Profitability must improve, and managers in all departments should be held responsible for this. Control should be exercised over all the aspects of the operation, and goals to be attained by all managers should be set and realized in 1996.
4. Also, a strong means to control and investigate food and beverages costs must take place.
5. A marketing plan in the sales department should take place in the first quarter of 1996, and it should be designed to increase the sales of rooms and food and beverages. Positive results must be seen shortly thereafter.

★ Property Analysis

This worksheet will provide a quick analysis of how your property is performing in comparison to the industry.

Worksheet	Your property	Comparison 1	Comparison 2	Comparison 3	Comparison 4	Comparison 5
Revenues						
Rooms						
Food						
Beverage						
Other Food and Beverage						
Telephone						
Minor-Operated						
Rentals & Other						
Total Revenue						
Operated Department Expense						
Rooms						
Food & Beverage						
Telephone						
Minor-Operated						
Total Operated Dept. Expense						
Operated Department Profit						
Rooms						
Food & Beverage						
Telephone						
Minor-Operated						
Rentals & Other						
Total Operated Dept. Profit						
Undistributed Expenses						
Administrative & General						
Payroll & Related						
Other						
Total						
Marketing						
Payroll & Related						
Other						
Total						
Energy						
Property Operation & Maintenance						
Total Undistributed Expenses						
Income Before Mngt. Fees & Fixed Chgs.						
Management Fees (Base & Incentive)						
Income Before Fixed Charges						
Fixed Charges						
Income Before Income Taxes						
Reserve for Capital Replacement						

★ Property Analysis

Ratio to Total Revenue (Sales)

This worksheet will provide a quick analysis of how your property is performing in comparison to the industry.

	Your property	Comparison 1	Comparison 2	Comparison 3	Comparison 4	Comparison 5
Revenues						
Rooms		60.0%	62.0%	63.5%	59.0%	
Food		24.0	25.5	23.0	26.0	
Beverage		10.0	8.7	11.00	10.0	
Other Food and Beverage		1.4	1.1	1.5	1.4	
Telephone		2.4	2.2	2.3	2.3	
Minor-Operated		1.0	2.1	1.2	1.0	
Rentals & Other		1.2	1.6	0.8	1.1	
Total Revenue		100.0	100.0	100.0	100.0	
Operated Department Expense						
Rooms		16.0	17.0	15.8	14.4	
Food & Beverage		29.0	32.5	28.7	30.4	
Telephone		2.0	2.1	2.4	2.3	
Minor-Operated		0.8	1.9	0.6	1.3	
Total Operated Dept Expense		47.0	49.0	42.8	46.0	
Operated Department Profit						
Rooms		45.0	45.1	49.0	43.2	
Food & Beverage		6.0	3.8	7.5	7.3	
Telephone		.4	0.1	<0.2>	0.1	
Minor-Operated		.2	.4	0.6	0.1	
Rentals & Other		.2	1.7	0.7	1.0	
Total Operated Dept. Profit		54.0	51.8	58.0	54.0	
Undistributed Expenses						
Administrative & General						
Payroll & Related		4.7	5.6	4.6	4.5	
Other		5.7	6.3	5.8	5.5	
Total		10.6	11.8	9.5	9.8	
Marketing						
Payroll & Related		2.0	2.1	1.9	1.9	
Other		5.0	3.8	4.6	4.6	
Total		7.0	5.8	5.9	6.3	
Energy		5.8	5.7	5.8	5.6	
Property Operation & Maintenance		5.1	5.3	5.2	5.2	
Total Undistributed Expenses		28.3	29.5	27.3	26.7	
Income Before Mngt. Fees & Fixed Chgs.		25.0	24.0	29.5	26.9	
Management Fees (Base & Incentive)		3.5	3.5	3.4	3.4	
Income Before Fixed Charges		22.8	22.0	26.9	25.4	
Fixed Charges		28.0	27.5	32.2	30.0	
Income Before Income Taxes		3.0%	<3.2>%	<4.6>%	<3.0>%	
Reserve for Capital Replacement		2.1	2.6	2.0	1.7	

Amounts and Percentages will not add due to the use of industry numbers reported by line by hotels.

★ **Property Analysis**

★ **Worksheet Analysis**

★ **Explanation**

Comparison to Industry Published Studies

Comparison 1. Ratio to Total Sales:
Hotels with 150 to 300 Rooms
Comparison 2. Ratio to Total Sales:
Independent Hotel
(Not Chain or "Flag" Affiliated)
Comparison 3. Ratio To Total Sales
Highway Location
Comparison 4. Ratio to Total Sales:
South Region

Section 3:

Room Demand: Area Occupancy Percentage

★ Instruction

Purpose:
Determine total rooms demanded in 1995 through 2000 in order to project occupancies for the area. Variations in different projections has also to be determined.

How to achieve that purpose:
- → Demographic and area data is available for this study. By using this data projections can be made.
- → Occupancy projections for each year could be determined by dividing total number of rooms demanded for each year, by the total number of rooms available for that same year. This will give the total area occupancy projected.
- → The Department of Transportation and The Chamber of Commerce provided some information related to room demand in 1993, 1994 and 1995. These numbers can be compared to the actual number of rooms occupied for 1993, 1994 and 1995; variations could be determined. These variations, depending on their importance, could be taken into consideration when projecting occupancy in future years.

★ Section 3
Room Demand
Suggested Solution

Projected Total Area Occupancy and Rooms Demanded						
	1995	1996	1997	1998	1999	2000
Industrial Park	—	—	3,466	6,934	10,400	10,400
Research Center	—	—	—	—	5,200	5,200
Highway Demand	40,150	43,800	47,450	51,100	54,750	58,400
Local Demand	32,850	36,500	40,150	43,800	47,450	51,100
Local Business Visitors	7,300	8,030	8,833	9,716	10,688	11,757
Total # of Rooms Demanded/Year	80,300	88,330	99,899	111,550	124,488	136,857
Total # of Rooms Available/Year	109,500	109,500	164,250	164,250	164,250	164,250
Average Area Occupancy Percentage	73.3%	80.7%	60.8%	67.9%	78.2%	83.3%

★ Solution

Area Occupancy

In 1995, the actual area occupancy percentage for both Star Motel and Bay's Inn were as follows:

Star Motel	60%	200 room
Bay's Inn	90%	100 rooms

The actual number of rooms occupied was:

$$\text{Star Motel: } 200 \times 60\% \times 365 = 43{,}800$$
$$\text{Bay's Inn: } 100 \times 90\% \times 365 = \underline{32{,}850}$$
$$\text{Room Occupied/Year} \qquad 76{,}650$$

Therefore, the actual occupancy percentage was:

$$\frac{76{,}650}{109{,}500} = 70\% \text{ and not } 73.3\% \text{ as was}$$

predicted by the Department of Transportation and the Chamber of Commerce.

Consideration, then, should be taken as of these variations. We also should keep in mind that by the year 1999 or 2000, if the predicted demand keeps increasing, a new competitor aside from the Holinite Inn may enter the same market. It is customary that an area occupancy of 70% warrants feasibility studies to determine expansion of existing hotels and new hotel building.

Section 4:

Competitive Position

46   SECTION 4

★ Instruction

Purpose:
Determine and analyze the facilities that might compete with Star Motel.

How to achieve that purpose:
→   Find out about the competition. Who are they? What do they offer? Where does Star Motel stand regarding this competition?
→   Determine the number of rooms available for 1993–2000. Determine the number of rooms occupied for 1993-1995, and what is the share of each hotel.
→   Prepare a schedule of total rooms occupied per hotel, and total 1996 - 2000, assuming even distribution. Information needed to accomplish this section can be found in the beginning pages of the case study, Star Motel vs. competition and demographic and area data. Schedules should be prepared in a logical and comprehensive manner.
→   Discussion can be brief because section 5 will add more light to this study. At that time, occupancy forecast and competitive analysis can be made easier. (Section 5 in this report is the same as Section 9 in the case study).

★ Solution

Star Motel, at the present time, is competing with only the Bay's Inn: a one hundred room, no service facilities motel. Bay's Inn has a very clear position: a budget motel ($30.00 a night rate) that serves mainly the highway traffic. It appears that Star Motel has been trying to compete, wrongly, with Bay's Inn, as indicated by the $45.00 and $42.00 average room rates in 1993 and 1994, when Bay's Inn opened for business.

With the right decisions, and a good management team, Star Motel can easily outdo the Bay's Inn. This has not been the case so far, but things must change.

Another emerging competitor will be the all new Holinite Inn: a 150 room facility expected to open at the beginning of 1997. While there is little information available at this point about the services to be offered by this new hotel, early indications show that there will be direct competition between Star Motel and the Holinite Inn over rooms and banquet facilities available at both properties. That is an additional reason why 1996 should be a turning point at Star Motel, in order to live up to the new threat of increasing direct competition.

Total Rooms Available By All Three Competitors								
	1993	1994	1995	1996	1997	1998	1999	2000
Star Motel	73,000	73,000	73,000	73,000	73,000	73,000	73,000	73,000
Bay's Inn	—	18,250	36,500	36,500	36,500	36,500	36,500	36,500
Holinite Inn	—	—	—	—	54,750	54,750	54,750	54,750
Total Rooms Available	73,000	91,250	109,500	109,500	164,250	164,250	164,250	164,250

Total Rooms Occupied			
	1993	1994	1995
Star Motel	65,700 (100%)	54,750 (79%)	43,800 (57%)
Bay's Inn	—	14,720 (21%)	32,850 (43%)
Total Rooms Occupied	65,700 (100%)	69,470 (100%)	76,650 (100%)

Projected Total Rooms Occupied (Share of the Market)						
	Occupancy:	1996	Even Distribution 1997	1998	1999	2000
Star Motel	44.5%	58,877	44,455	49,640	57,177	60,901
Bay's Inn	22.2%	29,443	22,178	24,764	28,524	30,382
Holinite Inn	33.3%	0	33,266	37,146	42,787	45,574
Total Rooms Demanded	100%	88,330	99,899	111,550	128,488	136,857
Total Room Occupancy		80.7%	60.8%	67.9%	78.2%	83.3%

*Comments on this section are located in Section 5.

Section 5:

Room Occupancy Forecast

★ Instruction

Purpose:
Determine room demand by day of the week. Room demand must be translated into occupancy percentages, and number of rooms demanded.

How to achieve that purpose:
→ Follow the schedule given in the case study. Omit Holinite Inn because it will not open until 1997. Project occupancies, based on highway traffic by day of the week; business demand by day of the week.
→ The average occupancy of the area and in each hotel must coincide with the average room occupancies projected in the previous section.
→ Multiply occupancies times rooms available in order to determine number of rooms occupied in each hotel per day, as well as in the area.
→ In forecasting these occupancies, take into consideration the guests who might choose Star Motel as opposed to Bay's Inn, as well as the guests who might choose Bay's Inn as opposed to Star Motel. We agree that information regarding these forecasts is very limited.
→ Once this is completed, competitive analysis can be better emphasized based on what we have learned in doing these charts. At this point, looking at all rooms demanded, forecasts and occupancies will be very helpful.

★ Solution

1996 Room Occupancy: By Day of the Week Occupancy Percentage			
Day	**Area Occupancy**	**Star Motel** (200 Rms)	**Bay's Inn** (100 Rms)
Monday	82%	79.8%	86.4%
Tuesday	83%	79.8%	82.2%
Wednesday	85%	82.7%	76.9%
Thursday	86%	83.7%	83.2%
Friday	73%	71.0%	89.5%
Saturday	78%	75.9%	86.4%
Sunday	79%	76.8%	90.6%
Average Occupancy	80.7%	78.5%	85%

The preceding two charts indicate weekly occupancy for both the Star Motel and the Bay's Inn; they are based on total area rooms demanded.

Star Motel

It is somewhat difficult to forecast Star Motel's daily occupancy since we do not have any records from previous years.

But based on total areas demand, Star Motel has the potential to attract most local demand and most local business visitors, in addition to the same highway traffic demand.

It is assumed that during the weekdays, occupancy will be higher than weekends, since business persons will be staying at Star Motel during the weekdays.

Also, occupancy during high traffic periods on Interstate 95 will be higher.

Bay's Inn

Bay's Inn occupancy is easier to forecast due to the fact that most of its occupants will be guests seeking lower rates, usually motorists looking for bargain prices. Therefore, weekends, and weekdays around the weekends are likely to have higher occupancies.

1996 Room Occupancy Forecast: By Day Of The Week Room Occupied			
Day	Area Rooms Occupied	Star Motel	Bay's Inn
Monday	246	160	83
Tuesday	246	160	82
Wednesday	255	165	77
Thursday	258	167	83
Friday	219	142	90
Saturday	234	152	86
Sunday	237	154	91
Average Rooms Occupied	242	157	85
Total Rooms Occupied/Year	88,330	57,305	31,025

★ Room Demand and Occupancy Analysis

In 1995, Bay's Inn managed to capture 43% of the total market, (or 10% higher than its even distribution share of the market), even though it has half the number of room as the Star Motel.

This is an indication that they either offer a product attractive to the market, or that the Star Motel is building a reputation obliging guests to look for another alternative rather than staying at their hotel. These two factors should be considered carefully by Star Motel management.

In order to succeed, Star Motel must capture its lost business from 1996, and should strive for at least 45% share of the market of the total rooms demanded in 1998.

In 1995, Star Motel had a 57% share of the market, while it should have had at least 67%. In 1998, Holinite Inn will most probably be the competition going after the same segment of the market as Star Motel. Both offer a similar product, and most likely would offer the same rates, or prices in their food and banquet facilities.

The most positive aspect of this room demand and occupancy analysis is that if the projections of a 10% yearly increase in room demand come true, Star Motel would be likely to benefit the most, due to its large number of rooms available.

Section 6:

Star Motel Characteristics

★ Instruction

Purpose:
Define the Motel's strong points.
Define the Motel's weak points.
Determine improvements that must be implemented.

How to achieve that purpose:
→ The order of priority will be done in a future section (Section 8). At this point it is better to simply indicate Star Motel's characteristics.
→ Based on our findings, ratio analysis and rooms demand, what Star Motel has to offer, ten positive strong points can be concluded, based on location, community, facilities, size, services, etc. . . . Ten negative points can be concluded based on occupancy, sales, income, marketing, costs, operations, policies and competition. Ten improvements could be implemented, based on marketing plan, standards, investigations, reductions of costs, improvement of occupancies and improvements of sales.

★ Solution

Ten Positive Characteristics of Star Motel

1. Its location in a community where substantial growth is expected.
2. Its location near an important Interstate highway which provides an important volume of business to the community.
3. Its banquet facilities.
4. Its meeting facilities which will be one of the main causes in attracting visitors and in selling rooms.
5. Its large size (number of rooms available).
6. Its ability to offer a higher level of service and amenities to customers than other competitors.
7. Its dining and cocktail facilities.
8. Its recreational facilities (tennis, swimming pool, etc. . . .).
9. Its stores.
10. Its important parking facilities which are able to contain a large number of cars.

Ten Negative Characteristics of Star Motel

1. Declining occupancy and declining sales per available room.
2. Operating at a loss for the past two years.
3. Lack of effective marketing strategy.
4. High costs of food and beverage.
5. No comprehensive accounting system, nor profit planning.
6. Lack of control over labor and energy costs.
7. Large food and beverage inventories.
8. Lack of control over credit policies.
9. Guests seem to be going elsewhere. This must be due to a lack of service, quality and unestablished standards for guests' satisfaction.
10. Holinite Inn could be a real danger if things continue in this same manner.

Ten Suggestions to Improve Operations and Deficiencies in 1996

1. Develop a marketing plan to improve sales and occupancy.
2. Implement standards and procedures in both food and beverage areas in order to control costs of production.
3. Management team must be investigated and evaluated in order to determine causes of deficiencies.
4. Training must be planned and executed at all levels.

5. A comprehensive accounting system must be established. Budgets must be planned and variances must be investigated.
6. Credit collection policies must be efficiently established.
7. Managers must forecast future events and plan them in order to reduce payroll and related costs.
8. Inventories should be reduced, and receiving and issuing procedures must be followed and adhered to.
9. P.O.M. and energy costs must be investigated and new policies must be implemented in order to reduce costs.
10. A sound operation has to be built and everyone in Star Motel is required to participate in this effort.

Section 7:

Marketing Plan and Competitive Position

★ Instruction

Purpose:
To develop and implement the most effective marketing plan that will increase revenues and profit.

How to achieve that purpose:
→ First, by determining the Motel's target markets based on what the target needs and what the Motel has to offer.
→ The Motel's Product, promotional efforts, position and price must be structured in order to accommodate that target market.
→ Sections 6 and 7 in the case study will be done together in this section since position is part of the marketing plan.
→ Finally, implementation of this plan will be executed in Section 8 of this report.

★ Solution

Marketing Plan

Star Motel's marketing plan should detail the projected activities of the organization. The following factors should be determined:

1. Who is involved?
2. Who is the motel's target market?
3. What does the motel have to propose to each target mark?
4. How much is the budget?

On the other hand, an overall program for selecting specific market segments, called a marketing strategy should be added in order to satisfy those guests through the careful use and analysis of the elements of the marketing mix. This marketing mix, is the set of controllable marketing variables that the motel blends to produce the response it wants in its target market. This concept held in planning marketing strategies, chooses what we can do to influence demand and attract guests. The many activities and possibilities can be brought about in four groups of variables:

1. Product
2. Promotion
3. Positioning and
4. Price

At Star Motel, there is no evidence that these variables have been considered as a total marketing package. Therefore, all these variables are to change.

Product Strategy

The product refers to the quality of services, features, facilities and amenities offered by the Star Motel. Its name and size are also parts of the product.

Star Motel has failed to respond to customers' needs for new and diversified services to the proper customer market. As we have seen earlier in the report, Star Motel has been trying to compete with Bay's Inn lower rates, while many potential customers in the community are more likely to prefer a service-oriented facility.

It is to these customers that Star Motel should address itself by making the most of its existing facilities, and in the near future by renovating and modifying these same facilities.

All evidence points out that the market is there, well and alive, and willing to pay for the product. But the product is not there, and only Star Motel is able to provide it.

Promotion Strategy

Promotion stands for the various activities that should be undertaken by Star Motel to communicate the merits of its product, and to persuade its market to buy it.

Promotion is an important part of the overall marketing strategy. Promotion strategy has four components:

1. **Advertising:** Star Motel, in this field, should undertake the following steps:
    → Newspapers and magazines advertising in local issues.
    → Advertising in specialized and business trade magazines in order to reach the business visitors.
    → Billboards, lit on I-95 for travelers.
    → Advertising in the AAA tour books.

2. **Personal Selling:** This could be done by questionnaire analysis utilized to provide the necessary data in developing the promotional strategy. The questionnaire analysis can be aimed at finding present guests' needs and wants, and help in promoting them. Also a registration analysis can provide an understanding of the guests' geographical origins which can aid in allocating advertising and promotional expenses to those areas where return will be greater. The results of both analyses can provide a list of potential guests, and combined with a knowledge of operational capacities can help in designing promotional appeals for each segment of the market.

3. **Publicity:** This should be done in order to promote Star Motel in the community. Some of these activities are:
    → Charity events.
    → Educational seminars.
    → Food and beverage seminars, including well known personalities.
    → Family planning, weight control, etc. . . .
    → Sponsoring sports events.

4. **Sales Promotions:** These include:
    → Live entertainment
    → Family brunch
    → Happy hour
    → Ladies night
    → Special nights—Recurrent and special occasions
    → Family weekend rate, to increase occupancy during the weekends.

Lists of potential guests must be developed in order to design a promotional strategy. Public relations have to be implemented, and post sales services such as comment cards, an 800 number, and thorough policy of follow-through based on guests' feedback are all a must. This would be very beneficial to the Star Motel.

Positioning Strategy

Positioning is a psychological activity in which Star Motel chooses to undertake to put positive knowledge and attitudes towards the product or service in the guests' minds.

Star Motel's services are unique (since competition does not have them). These services should be promoted in a way that the motel's image is perceived through them. This would build a gap that the competition can not cross.

Star Motel should enforce this image by community relations and public relations. An image of high profile, able to accommodate middle income people should be built around the Star's name, and make it stand up among the competition. Everyone should know what the Star has to offer. Its quality services have to be promoted and guests should know how to benefit from them.

Price Strategy

Star Motel's rate structure should be carefully reviewed based on:

1. Break even point.
2. The rate of return.
3. What the market is willing to pay for it.

4. Operational and profit perspective.
5. How pricing is used to create the perception value.
6. A close look at the competition.

Star Motel must succeed in matching its services to the proper target market, because its cost structure cannot sustain offering rates close to those offered by the Bay's Inn.

Depending upon the seasonality and the market outlook, a price structure indicating the various rates should be developed in detail, including the official posted rates. The price structure should also include the seasonal changes in these rates.

Section 8:

Timetable for Implementation—1996

★ Instruction

Purpose:
To determine what should be done in 1996 in order to improve the Motel's performance.

How to achieve that purpose:
- → Start February 1, 1996.
- → Determine priorities.
- → Previous sections will help determine these priorities. For example, when reporting the Motel's characteristics, 10 items citing the negative aspects of the Motel will have to be reversed and dates to implement steps reversing these aspects could be put in order in this section. Also the 10 suggestions of improvements can be listed here.
- → At this point, the marketing plan should also be implemented.
- → For the most part, items that have to be implemented came from the previous two sections. So based on those two sections, an action plan for 1996 will be implemented in order of priority.

★ Solution

Tuesday 10:00 A.M. weekly management and department head meeting.

February 1996:
1. Managers' meeting: set guidelines for operations for 1996. New procedures for each department.
3. Employees' meetings in each department: get feedback about causes of deficiencies. Determine training needs.
4. Department heads must act on these feedbacks and investigate and correct the problems.
15. Set new standards. Implement control in food and beverage area.
15. Maintenance should report on causes of high P.O.M. and energy costs.
20. Training sessions should start.
28. Accounting department should be re-organized, and forecasts and budgets should be in place.

March:
1. Marketing plan should be implemented.
2. Plans for all departments should be finalized by the General Manager, and executed by every department head.
30. Managers' meeting to check progress in each department. Statements should be produced based on daily operations.

April:
2. Check progress with marketing plan.
2. Start to develop Guests' File: names, origins, professions, . . .
2. Comments cards in all rooms and food and beverage facilities.
18. First quarter statements of operations should be completed and compared to last year's first quarter. Written evaluation of the results should be prepared by controller and each department head.
30. Check progress on the comprehensive accounting system.

May:
2. Plan for events in the Motel to attract publicity.
30. Some of these plans should be finalized, scheduled and implemented.

June:
1. Check progress in all departments.
2. By now the public should be aware of the Star's new image.
15. Evaluate results of marketing plans, make modifications and adjustments.
30. Check on effectiveness of the training program.

July:
8. Check statements of the second quarter. Compare them to the first quarter. They must show improvement.
15. Final implementation of new revisions of food and beverage cost control procedures.
15. Final implementations of comprehensive accounting system.
30. Meeting to discuss further implementation of marketing plan. Check progress up to present.

August:
1. Check progress in all departments; make necessary changes.
10. Obtain feedback from employees through meetings.
30. Obtain feedback from community through questionnaires.

September:
10. Discuss next year's budget.
15. Evaluate results of marketing plan; make necessary changes.
30. Department heads meet with General Manager and Controller to review departmental budgets.

October:
2. Meeting to review budget.
10. Become actively involved in the community.

November:
2. Meeting to review budget.
15. Formal submission of departmental operational performance reports to the General Manager and Controller.
30. Check performances in each department.

December:
1. Final approval of budget.
5. Hold charity event for Christmas.
15. Evaluate results of the marketing plan and make necessary changes.
24-31. Celebrate Christmas, New Years, and the rebirth of the Star Motel, managers and employees together.

Section 9:

Pro-Forma Comparative Statements of Operations 1995-1996

★ Instruction

Purpose:
To prepare a projected statement of operations to be used as a measure of operational performances in 1996.

How to achieve that purpose:
→ Based on 1995 performances and the improvements that have to be implemented starting February, 1996, assumptions will have to be made.
→ These assumptions are presented as exhibits from A to M. The implementation of a new marketing plan, for example, will increase sales in the rooms, food and beverages departments. The implementation of better control measures will likely decrease costs, payroll and related expenses.
→ In this section, a student cannot be wrong in projecting a number for any account, but when they should do this, through assumptions, present in a logical manner what is likely to happen in each and every account in order to project new income for the coming year, 1996. They should also stay as close as possible to the projections for the room occupancies made in the previous sections, the marketing plan, and the implementation of standards to be followed in every department. Here logic is the name of the game.

★ Exhibit A
1996 Room Sales

Average Room Rate: $42.00
Number of Rooms Available: 200 rooms
Occupancy Expected to increase to: 78.5% (as projected in Section 5).
Total rooms Occupied in 1996: 57,305 rooms (as projected in Section 5).
1996 Room Sales = 57,305 x $42 = $2,406,810

In regard to this department, Star Motel's primary goal should be to increase room occupancy and revenue without changing the room rates. The sales department's marketing plan must have this objective. This plan should attract guests from Bay's Inn on the basis of the services available at Star Motel; Star Motel must attract the greatest part of the newly coming customers to the area (the business visitors section and the growing local demand). Analyze in detail the room rate justification coupled with the higher occupancy. What will Bay's Inn marketing strategy be as their occupancy drops from 90% to 85%? How will you combat their counter marketing plan?

★ Exhibit B
1996 Payroll and Related Expenses and
Other Expenses of Rooms Department

The Star Motel's comparative statements of operations shows that payroll and related expenses in the room department have increased sharply from 1993 to 1994, from 15.65% in 1993, to 23.20% in 1994. A workable objective for 1996 is to bring this percentage back to its 1993 level as a first step; in 1997 and later, a thorough analysis should reduce this percentage even further or justify each employee.

The same could be said about other expenses in the room department. These percentages increased from 6.83% in 1993 to 11.22% in 1994. As a first step in 1996 these expenses should be brought back to their previous level.

This should not be done at the expense of guests satisfaction, but through adequate employees' scheduling and cost control in the room department.

Budget Objective	1996
Room Sales	= $2,406,810
Payroll & Related Expenses (15.65%)	= $ 376,666
Other Expenses (6.83%)	= $ 164,385
Total Expenses	$ 541,051

★ Exhibit C
1996 Food and Beverage Sales

Despite a decrease in customers count in the last two years, resulting from a decrease in occupancy percentage, the food and beverage department succeeded in keeping its level of sales unchanged. The Bay's Inn has no food and beverage service. This was not accomplished through smart decisions taken by the department, but because of the availability of demand for these services. These results indicate that this department could generate a high volume of sales if plans are developed in this direction. Live entertainment, happy hours, ladies and special nights, and quality service are guaranteed to increase sales in the food and beverage department dramatically.

Based on this marketing plan and on the forecast of increased occupancy in 1996 of 18.5%, food and beverage sales must, as a result, increase by an average of 20% or better.

1995 Food Sales	=$1,200,000	
1996 Food Sales	=$1,200,000 + 20%	= $1,440,000
1995 Beverage Sales	=$ 480,000	
1996 Beverage Sales	=$ 480,000 + 20%	= 576,000
1996 Total Food and Beverage Sales		= $2,016,000

★ Exhibit D
1996 Cost of Sales
Food and Beverage

Food cost over the last three years increased from an already high cost of 46% in 1993 to 69.45% in 1994, to an unbelievable level of 74.60% in 1995. In 1996, the utmost control must be exercised over this area.

Standard recipes, portion control, improved purchasing, receiving, storing, issuing procedures and other controls must be implemented. Preparation and holding should be closely monitored. Spoilage, waste and theft are to be located, investigated and brought to light. Inventory must be reduced to avoid spoilage and proper methods of keeping inventories must be implemented.

As the first step, food cost should not exceed the 40% level. Further reduction must take place to reduce it to 35% in 1996. Do not radically make changes without having a sound basis and monitoring results daily and by shift. Don't lose the customers you now have.

1996 Food Sales	= $1,440,000	
1996 Food Cost	= $1,440,000 x 40%	= $576,000

The same procedures must be implemented in the beverage area. The fluctuating beverage cost in the last three years is another indication of the abnormality of this cost. Investigations and control procedures must take place as early as February 1996. Beverage cost must be brought down to a maximum of 25% in 1996, and be further improved in 1997.

1996 Beverage Sales	= $576,000	
1996 Beverage Cost	= $576,000 x 25%	=$144,000
1996 Total Food and Beverage Costs		=$720,000

★ Exhibit E
1996 Other Food and Beverage Income

This account has been decreasing over the last two years. An increase in other than food and beverage banquet services, catering, and public activities must increase sales in this area. This includes room rentals, equipment rentals, music, flowers, decorations, etc.

Local business meetings demand is:

1995:	10-20 persons	= 104 meetings/year
	30-40 persons	= 156 meetings/year
	50 persons	= 52 meetings/year
	Number of persons	= 9,620 customers/year
1996:	10-20 persons	= 114 meetings/year
	30-40 persons	= 172 meetings/year
	50 persons	= 57 meetings/year
	Number of persons	= 10,582 customers/year

A plan to attract these business meetings would have a great impact on income in this area, as well as on room sales. These meetings should be encouraged to consume foods and beverages and this could be done based on the study of these customers' actual and future needs. This must be accomplished as soon as possible.

As a start, income in this area should increase from $30,000 in 1995 to at least $60,000 in 1996.

★ Exhibit F
1996 Payroll and Related Expenses and Other Expenses
In Food and Beverage Department

Payroll and Related Expenses

As we have already mentioned in Exhibit B, control over staffing and scheduling in the food and beverage area should also take place. A workable objective of 30% must be implemented in 1996 and reduced further in future years.

One of the most effective policies is to develop job lists, job breakdowns, job descriptions and performance standards for every job in the Motel. This should be based on a thorough study and analysis of every task to be performed and the standards to be reached, and the application of a training program where it is needed. This is the best way to control payroll expenses.

1996 Food and Beverage Sales	= $2,016,000	
1996 Payroll and Related Expenses	= $2,016,000 x 30%	= $604,800

Other Expenses

Breakage control, coordination between kitchen, bar and dining rooms, better efficiency and control procedures, must bring the level of these other expenses to 7% in 1996.

1996 Other Expenses	= $2,016,000 x 7%	= $141,120

★ Exhibit G
1996 Telephone

New technology and government regulations have made the telephone department a profitable department in most hotels. Star Motel is still losing money in this area; this could be due to a lack of knowledge about the new technology by the management in the Motel. A new system, if this is the problem, must be installed. (Payback for these systems is very short, and could reverse this unprofitable trend.)

Since a new system might not be installed in 1996, loss in this department might persist in the order of 1% of room revenues. But in 1997, this must be a revenue generating department.

1996 Room Sales	= $2,406,810	
1996 Telephone (Loss)	= $2,406,810 x 1%	= ($24,068)

★ Exhibit H
1996 Minor Operating Departments

As room revenue is expected to increase in 1996, consequently, revenue from minor operating departments will also increase by approximately the same percentage.

     1996 Minor Operating Depts. = $24,000 + 15% Growth = $27,600

New ideas to increase sales in these departments should be thought over and examined, (vending machines, etc . . .).

★ Exhibit I
1996 General and Administrative
Payroll and Related Expenses
Other Expenses

Payroll and Related Expenses

This account kept at a level of 7% of room sales in 1993 and in 1994, but increased to 8.67% in 1995. A close look at this should have the ability to determine exactly what is the appropriate level of expense in this area. As an objective projected level of 7% in 1996 must be realized; then reduced further in 1997, after developing, as we mentioned earlier, job lists, job breakdowns, job descriptions and performance standards.

  1993 Room Sales   = $2,406,810
  1993 Administrative and General Payroll = $2,406,810 x 7% = $168,477
    and Related Expenses as % of R.S.

Other Expenses

The same tendency as above is detected in Other Expenses account; as a first this level of expense should be reduced to the 1993 level of 9%, then reduced further in 1997 after determining the causes of the discrepancies.

  1996 Room Sales   = $2,406,810
  1996 Adm. and General Other Expenses = $2,406,810 x 9% = $216,613

  1996 Total Administrative and General   = $385,090

★ Exhibit J
1996 Marketing

Over the last three years, marketing expenses stayed in the 6% level, well above the industry average of 4%. This happened without any positive result reflected in the activities of other departments. This means that this account was nothing more than a drain.

In 1996, due to the undertaking of the major marketing plan, an increase of approximately 4% to 10% level of room sales must be largely sufficient to provide funds to implement the plan in order to increase room occupancy, food and beverage activity, and business meetings.

    1996 Room Sales = $2,406,810
    1996 Marketing   = $2,406,810 x 10% = $240,681

★ Exhibit K
1996 Energy

Star Motel has maintained over the last three years an energy expense level of 7%, which is 2.4% over the industry average. As a first step to reduce the Motel's energy cost, a 1% decrease must occur in this account in 1996; it should then be further reduced to the industry average in 1997.

    1996 Energy   = $2,406,810 x 6%   = $144,409

1996 Property and Maintenance

It is true that Star Motel is growing older, and as a result, P.O.M. costs to room sales might increase over the years. However, the speed at which this increase has occurred, is far above the normal level (75% increase over a two year period is abnormal.) In 1995 the cost was three times more than the industry average. Management must investigate and bring appropriate changes. In 1996, due to increased occupancy, a large reduction in this account might not be attainable. However an 8% cost to room sales must be appropriate in 1996, then reduced further in 1997.

    1996 P.O.M.   = $2,406,810 x 8%   = $192,545

★ Exhibit L
1996 Municipal Taxes

These taxes have been increasing over the last three years. It is anticipated that this trend will continue in 1996 since no renovations or improvements in the property will take place.

The trend indicates that these taxes might reach the level of 8% of room sales in 1996. This is an increase of 1.30% over 1995. A real estate tax appeal should be investigated by the motel's attorney.

    1996 Municipal Taxes   = $2,406,810 x 8%   = $192,545

1996 Insurance

The cost of insurance has been increasing at a rate that is difficult to bear. Management should be alarmed, and must review carefully their insurance policy and the causes of this increase.

A risk management plan must be implemented in 1996 in order to reduce insurance costs. But as an estimate for 1996, the cost for insurance might reach the 5% level. But in 1997 this percentage must be reduced dramatically.

    1996 Insurance   = $2,406,810 x 5%   = $120,341

    1996 Total Taxes and Insurance   = $372,886

★ Exhibit M
1996 Interest Expense

Star Motel pays a very high amount of interest, 40.28% of room sales in 1995. Increased room sales in 1996 will decrease this percentage to about 30% of room sales. However, alternatives of financing at cheaper rates must be implemented.

    1996 Interest Expense   = $2,406,810 x 30%   = $722,043

Depreciation and Amortization

The depreciation amount of $270,000 will not increase in 1996. Any purchase of new fixed assets will be depreciated on the straight line basis. There is no remaining amortization.

1996 Depreciation	$270,000
1996 Amortization	$0
1996 Total Depreciation and Amortization	$270,000

1996 Income Tax

The trends indicate that Star Motel's income tax rate is about 35.77% of net income before taxes. It is expected that the Motel in 1996 will not benefit from any tax refund as income generated will be much higher than in 1994 and 1995. There is an effective 40% tax rate for 1996.

1996 Income Before Tax	= $226,717	
1996 Income Tax	= $226,717 x 40%	= $90,687

Star Motel
Pro-Forma Comparative Statements of Operations
For the Year Ending December 31.

Page 1 of 2

Items	Amounts			Percentages (1)			Exhibit#	Line#	Line Combinations
	1996	1995	Difference	1996	1995	Difference			
Rooms								1	
Sales	$2,406,810	$1,800,000	$+606,810	100.00%	100.00%	0.00PT	A	2	
Departmental Expenses								3	
Payroll and Related Expenses	$376,666	$420,000	$-43,334	15.65%	23.33%	-7.68PT	B	4	
Other Expenses	$164,385	$210,000	$-45,615	6.83%	11.67%	-4.84PT	B	5	
Total Expenses	$541,051	$630,000	$-88,949	22.48%	35.00%	-12.52PT	B	6	4 + 5
Departmental Income - Rooms	$1,865,759	$1,170,000	$+695,749	77.52%	65.00%	+12.52PT		7	2 - 6
Food & Beverage(1)								8	
Sales								9	
Food	$1,440,000	$1,200,000	$+240,000	71.43%	71.43%	0.00PT	C	10	
Beverage	$576,000	$480,000	$+96,000	28.57%	28.57%	0.00PT	C	11	
Total Sales	$2,016,000	$1,680,000	$+336,000	100.00%	100.00%	0.00PT	C	12	10 + 11
Cost of Sales								13	
Food Cost	$576,000	$895,200	$-319,200	40.00%	74.60%	-34.60PT	D	14	
Beverage Cost	$144,000	$264,000	$-120,000	25.00%	55.00%	-30.00PT	D	15	
Total Costs	$720,000	$1,159,200	$-439,200	71.00%	69.00%	-33.29PT	D	16	14 + 15
Gross Profit	$1,296,000	$520,800	$+775,200	64.29%	31.00%	+33.29PT	D	17	12 - 16
Other Income - Net	$60,000	$30,000	$+30,000	2.98%	1.79%	+1.19PT	E	18	
Gross Profit and Other Income	$1,356,000	$550,800	$+805,200	67.26%	32.79%	+34.47PT		19	17 + 18
Departmental Operating Expenses								20	
Payroll and Related Expenses	$604,800	$688,800	$-84,000	30.00%	41.00%	-11.00PT	F	21	
Other Expenses	$141,120	$168,000	$-26,888	7.00%	10.00%	-3.00PT	F	22	
Total Departmental Expenses	$745,920	$856,800	$-110,880	37.00%	51.00%	-14.00PT		23	21 + 22
Departmental Income - Food and Beverage	$610,080	$[306,000]	$+916,080	30.26%	<18.21%>	+48.47PT		24	19 - 23
Telephone [Loss]	$[24,068]	$[24,000]	$-68	<1.00%>	<1.33%>	+.33PT	G	25	
Minor Operating Departments	$27,600	$24,000	$+3,600	1.15%	1.33%	-.18PT	H	26	
Store Rentals	$30,000	$30,000	$00	1.25%	1.67%	-.42PT		27	No change budgeted in 1996
								28	

Star Motel
Pro-Forma Comparative Statements of Operations
For the Year Ending December 31.

Items	Amounts			Percentages (1)			Exhibit#	Line#	Line Combinations
	1996	1995	Difference	1996	1995	Difference			
Operated Departments								29	
Net Income	$2,509,371	$894,000	$+1,615,311	4.26%	49.67%	+54.59PT		30	7 + 24 + 25 + 26 + 27
Undistributed Operating Expenses								31	
Administrative and General								32	
Payroll and Related Expenses	$168,477	$156,000	$+12,477	7.00%	8.67%	-1.67PT	I	33	
Other Expenses	$216,613	$192,000	$+24,613	9.00%	10.67%	-1.67PT	I	34	
Total Administrative and General	$385,090	$348,000	$+37,090	6.00%	19.33%	-13.33PT	I	35	33 + 34
Marketing	$240,681	$113,400	$+127,281	0.00%	6.30%	+3.70PT	J	36	
Energy	$144,409	$126,000	$+18,409	6.00%	7.00%	-1.00PT	K	37	
P.O.M.	$192,545	$186,000	$+6,545	8.00%	10.33%	-2.33PT	K	38	
Total Undistributed								39	
Operating Expenses	$962,725	$773,400	$+189,325	10.00%	42.97%	-2.97PT		40	35 + 36 + 37 + 38
Net Income Before Fixed Charges	$1,546,646	$120,600	$+1,426,046	64.26%	6.70%	+57.56PT		41	30 - 40
Fixed Charges								42	
Municipal Taxes	$192,545	$120,600	$+71,945	8.00%	6.70%	+1.30PT	L	43	
Insurance	$120,341	$80,000	$+40,341	5.00%	4.44%	+.56PT	L	44	
Total Taxes and Insurance	$312,886	$200,600	$+112,286	13.00%	11.14%	+1.86PT	L	45	43 + 44
Net Income Before Interest								46	
and Depreciation	$1,233,760	$[80,000]	$+1,313,760	51.26%	4.44%	+55.70PT		47	41 - 45
Interest Expense	$722,043	$725,000	$-2,951	30.00%	40.28%	-10.28PT	M	48	
Net Income Before Depreciation	$511,717	$[805,000]	$+1,316,717	21.26%	<44.72%>	+65.98PT		49	47 - 48
Depreciation and Amortization	$285,000	$285,000	$15,000	11.22%	<15.83%>	-4.61PT	M	50	
Net Income [Loss] Before Tax	$226,717	$[1,090,000]	$+1,331,717	10.04%	<60.56%>	+70.60PT		51	49 - 50
Provision for Income Tax [Refund] (2)	$96,687	$[390,000]	$+486,687	4.01%	<21.67%>	+25.68PT	M	52	
Net Income [Loss]	$145,030	$[700,000]	$+845,030	5.63%	<38.89%>	+44.92PT		53	51 - 52

(1) Percentages are to room sales except food and beverage percentages are to food and beverage sales.
PT is point difference between percentages.

Page 2 of 2

Section 10:

Pro-Forma Balance Sheet
Pro-Forma Statement of Cash Receipts and Disbursements
Pro-Forma "Quick Cash Flow" Statement

★ Instruction

Pro–Forma Balance Sheet 1996

Purpose:
To prepare a projected balance sheet to be used as a measure to improve the Motel's financial position.

How to achieve that purpose:
The ending Balance Sheet is the result of the following:

- → Beginning Balance Sheet
- → + and - Statement of Operations for the period
- → + and - Statement of Cash Receipts and Cash Disbursements for the period
- → Equals ending Balance Sheet

This is the foundation of double entry accounting. Here the ratios analyses done in previous sections must be very helpful, especially the ratios that originated from the balance sheet.

For example, we have seen in the liquidity ratios that current and quick ratios are decreasing rapidly, and we stated that this must be halted. Now is the time to state so. To increase or stabilize the current ratios, current assets have to increase or stabilize, and/or current liabilities have to decrease or stabilize. As we have projected earlier, revenues are expected to increase in 1996, therefore, current assets will increase, thus the current ratio will increase.

In regard to the quick ratio, and in order to improve it, one factor is inventory will have to decrease in favor of cash, thus increasing the quick ratio.

Also a measure of improving the Motel's liquid position, accounts receivable percentage, accounts receivable turnover and number of days sales uncollected will have to decrease in favor of more liquid current assets. This could be done by implementing better collection and credit policies, thus decreasing accounts receivable and increasing cash.

This cash increase, from all of these sources: increased sales; decreased inventory; and decreased accounts receivable, will permit the Motel to pay part of its current liabilities, and as a result, enhance further its liquid position.

Solvency and leverage ratios can also be improved by following the same methods as above: decreased liabilities and increased assets. This will ultimately lead to a better financial position.

Therefore, to have a clearer understanding of how to project a balance sheet, students should be aware of this importance, that the ratios are intricately connected with this projection and depending on how the student perceives the Motel's performances, the ratios should be based on that perception and as a result projected statements and balance sheets must agree with that perspective.

★ Instruction

Pro-Forma Statement of Cash Receipts and Disbursements 1996

Purpose:
To determine the Motel's ability to meet bills and debts payments when they are due, so averages and shortages in cash could be eliminated.

How to achieve that purpose:
Cash balance is the cash opening balance + cash receipts - cash disbursements. In Star Motel's case, no precise information is given regarding how much is bought on credit, and how much is bought and paid for in cash. Therefore, the student should be encouraged to be as realistic as possible. The student should set a standard for what is best for the Motel to pay and receive in cash and in receivables. He or she should also have an understanding of what happens in the real world regarding these transactions. Then he or she will try to draw a line between the two alternatives that will be used as a cash flow measure.

Students should understand that in case of cash shortages, steps should be taken to eliminate those shortages, borrowing, selling of stocks, etc. . . . And in case of cash overages, steps should be taken, including reduction of liabilities, investments, or used for improvements in the physical plant.

★ Instruction

Pro-Forma Quick Cash Flow Statement 1996

Purpose:
To determine changes in working capital.

How to achieve this purpose:
All the figures are found in the balance sheets differences for 1995 and 1996, and the statements of operations in 1996.

★ Solution

	Star Motel Pro-Forma Comparative Balance Sheets For the Years ending December 31.		
Items	**1996**	**1995**	**Difference**
Assets			
Current Assets			
Cash	$878,900	$100,000	$+778,900
Accounts Receivable	$225,817	$510,000	$-284,183
Income Tax Receivable	—	$390,000	$-390,000
Inventory (1995, Food 40%,Bvg.60%)	$41,000	$120,000	$-79,000
(1996, Food 50%,Bvg.50%)			
Prepaid Insurance	$15,000	$15,000	—
Total Current Assets	$1,160,717	$1,135,000	$+25,717
Fixed Assets			
Land (20 Acres)	$600,000	$600,000	—
Building (40 years, s/l)	$6,600,000	$6,600,000	—
Furnitures and Equipment (10 years, s/l)	$1,050,000	$1,050,000	—
Total Fixed Assets	$8,250,000	$8,250,000	—
Less: Accumulated Depreciation	$1,620,000	$1,350,000	+270,000
Net Value Fixed Assets	$6,630,000	$6,900,000	-270,000
Other Assets			
Deposits	$30,000	$30,000	—
Total Assets	$7,820,717	$8,065,000	$-244,283
Liabilities and Stockholders' Equity			
Current Liabilities			
Note Payable Demand 15%	—	$300,000	$-300,000
Accounts Payable	$321,000	$408,000	$-87,000
Accrued Expenses	$60,000	$60,000	—
Income Taxes Payable	$90,687	—	$+90,687
Current Portion - Mortgage	$93,000	$84,000	$+9,000
Total Current Liabilities	$564,687	$852,000	$-287,313
Long-Term Debt - Mortgage 14%	$6,105,000	$6,198,000	$-93,000
Total Liabilities	$6,669,687	$7,050,000	$-380,313
Stockholders' Equity			
Common Stock, $10 Par	$100,000	$100,000	—
Capital Surplus	$900,000	$900,000	—
Retained Earnings	$151,030	$15,000	$+136,030
Total Stockholders' Equity	$1,151,030	$1,015,000	$+136,030
Total Liabilities and Stockholders' Equity	$7,820,717	$8,065,000	$-244,283

Star Motel
Pro-Forma Statement of Cash Receipts and Disbursements
For the year Ending Dec. 31, 1996

Item	Amount
Opening Cash Balance—Jan. 1	$100,000
Receipts	
Room Cash Revenue	$2,283,925
Food and Beverage Cash Revenue	$1,913,068
Collect on Accounts Receivable	$900,000
Other Income	$60,000
Minor Operating Departments	$27,600
Store Rental	$30,000
Total Available	$5,314,593
Disbursements	
Cash Food Cost	$560,000
Cash Beverage Cost	$135,000
Other Cash Expenses	$473,118
Note Payable Paid	$300,000
Accounts Payable Paid—Net	$88,000
Current Portion Paid on Mortgage	$93,000
Payroll and Related Expenses	$1,149,943
Telephone Loss	$24,068
Marketing	$240,681
Energy	$144,409
P.O.M.	$192,545
Municipal Taxes	$192,545
Insurance	$120,341
Interest	$722,043
Total	$4,435,693
Closing Cash Balance—Dec. 31	$878,900

Pro-Forma Statement of Cash Flow
For the Year Ending December 31, 1996

Estimated Cash Flow from Operations		
Net income after Tax	$145,030	
Add Back, Depreciation	270,000	
Total from Operations	$415,030	
Add New Financing	—	
Total Cash Inflow		$415,030
Less: Cash Outflow		
Principal Payments on Debt—Provided	$93,000	
Capital Improvements	—	
Dividends	$9,000	
Other	—	
Total Cash Outflow		$102,000
Cash Flow Excess or (Deficiency)		$313,030

Section 11:

Pro-Forma Statements of Cash Receipts and Cash Disbursements By Month

★ Instruction

Pro-Forma Statement of Cash Receipts and Disbursements By Month

Purpose:

To determine the Motel's ability to meet daily, weekly, monthly bills, other recurrent and one-time obligations and debt payments when they are due, so shortages and overages in cash can be planned in advance with the intent of eliminating a cash crisis.

How to achieve this purpose:

This is accomplished the same way as the cash flow statement in the previous section. But every account should be broken into twelve parts on a monthly basis. Here the student must be aware and be able to differentiate between a high, low and shoulder months. It is true that not much information about such is given, but some assumptions can be made.

By completing this statement, you must be able to see when cash is needed to pay debts and when it is necessary to borrow money. This has to be determined even though much of the information necessary to deal with decisions is not readily available or known.

Star Motel
Pro-Forma Statement of Cash Receipts and Disbursements**
For the Year Ending December 31, 1996

Item	Jan.*	Feb.	March	April	May	June	July	Aug.	Sept.	Oct.	Nov.	Dec.	Total
Opening Cash Balance	100,000	31,716	<26,568>	<32,302>	<3,204>	25,579	68,079	194,679	350,179	533,979	450,287	691,995	100,000
Receipts													
Room Revenue	120,000	120,000	135,000	150,000	170,000	185,000	200,000	210,000	226,000	242,000	252,000	273,925	2,283,925
Food & Bev. Revenue	110,000	110,000	120,000	130,000	137,000	150,000	162,000	175,000	187,000	198,000	210,000	224,068	1,913,068
Collection on Accounts Rec.	60,000	60,000	65,000	67,000	72,000	75,000	78,000	80,000	82,000	84,000	86,000	91,000	900,000
Other Income	1,800	1,800	2,200	3,000	4,000	4,600	5,300	6,000	6,700	7,400	8,100	9,100	60,000
Minor Oper. Depts.	1,500	1,500	1,700	1,800	2,000	2,200	2,300	2,500	2,700	2,900	3,100	3,400	27,600
Store Rental	2,500	2,500	2,500	2,500	2,500	2,500	2,500	2,500	2,500	2,500	2,500	2,500	30,000
Total	395,800	327,516	299,832	321,998	384,296	444,879	518,179	670,679	857,079	1,070,779	1,011,987	1,295,988	5,314,593
Disbursements													
Food Cost	74,600	72,000	65,000	58,000	48,000	45,000	42,000	38,000	34,600	30,000	26,400	26,400	560,000
Beverage Cost	22,000	20,000	16,000	14,000	12,000	10,000	8,000	7,000	7,200	6,700	5,800	6,300	135,000
Other Cash Expenses	47,500	47,500	44,000	42,000	42,000	40,000	37,000	35,000	35,700	34,000	34,000	34,418	473,118
Note Payable Paid	—	—	—	—	—	—	—	—	—	300,000	—	—	300,000
Accounts Payable Paid	—	—	—	—	38,000	50,000	—	—	—	—	—	—	88,000
Current Portion-Mtg.	—	—	—	—	—	—	—	—	—	—	—	93,000	93,000
Payroll and Related Exp.	105,400	100,000	92,000	92,000	92,000	92,000	93,000	94,000	95,000	96,000	97,000	101,543	1,1499,43
Telephone Loss	2,000	2,000	2,000	2,068	2,000	2,000	2,000	2,000	2,000	2,000	2,000	2,000	24,068
Marketing	9,450	9,450	14,000	18,000	24,000	24,000	24,000	24,000	24,000	24,000	24,000	21,781	240,681
Energy	10,500	10,500	9,000	9,000	10,000	10,800	11,500	12,500	13,600	15,000	15,000	17,009	144,409
P.O.M.	15,500	15,500	13,000	13,000	14,000	15,000	16,000	17,000	18,000	19,000	20,000	16,545	192,545
Municipal Taxes	10,050	10,050	10,050	10,050	10,050	15,000	17,000	18,000	20,000	22,000	24,000	26,295	192,545
Insurance	6,667	6,667	6,667	6,667	6,667	12,000	12,000	12,000	12,000	13,000	13,000	13,006	120,341
Interest	60,417	60,417	60,417	60,417	60,000	61,000	61000	61,000	61,000	58,792	58,792	58,791	722,043
Fixed Assets Additions	—	—	—	—	—	—	—	—	—	—	—	100,000	100,000
Total	364,084	35,4084	332,134	325,202	358,717	376,800	323,500	320,500	323,100	620,492	319,992	517,088	4,535,693
Closing Cash Balance	31,716	<26,568>	<32,302>	<3,204>	25,579	68,079	194,679	350,179	533,979	450,287	691,995	778,900	778,900

* Total Opening Cash Balance Denotes Cash Balance at Year Ended December 31, 1995 of $100,000.

** Amounts in dollars.

Section 12:

Quick Cash Flow Projections

★ Instruction

Quick Cash Flow Projection
1996, 1997, 1998, 1999, 2000

Purpose:
To plan for cash overages and shortages, and to indicate ability to meet obligations when they are due.

How to achieve that purpose:
- → Follow the format given initially. This format can be adjusted to fit your needs.
- → Determine cash inflow from operations from the figures already given in the projections of previous sections, (net income and depreciation).
- → Add new financing if applicable, (borrowing long-term debts, capitol leases, etc. . . .) and other inflows.
- → Deduct cash outflow: payments on long-term debts, capital expenditures and other outflows.
- → Capital expenditures were projected at $330,000 in 1997, subject to changes.
- → Expansion, and or borrowing will be, in part, based on the results of the cash flow excess or deficiency.

★ Solution

Star Motel
Pro-Forma Statement of Cash Flow
For the Years Ending December 31.

Items	Amounts				
	1996	1997	1998	1999	2000
Estimated Cash Inflow from Operations					
Net Income After Tax	$145,030	$376,217	$537,991	$831,122	$973,924
Add: Back Depreciation	270,000	270,000	270,000	270,000	270,000
Total from Operations	415,030	646,217	807,991	1,101,122	1,243,924
Add: New Financing	—	—	—	—	—
Total Cash Inflow	415,030	646,217	807,991	1,101,122	1,243,924
Less: Cash Outflow					
Principal Payments on Debt	93,000	124,000	165,000	220,000	293,000
Capital Improvements	—	330,000	—	—	—
Dividends	—	—	—	—	9,000
Total Cash Outflow	102,000	454,000	165,000	220,000	293,000
Cash Flow Excess or [Deficiency]	$313,030	$192,217	$642,991	$881,122	$950,924

Section 13:

Analysis of Pro-Forma Statements

88 SECTION 13

★ Instruction

Analysis Of Pro-Forma Statements

Purpose:
To set guidelines for management to follow in order to achieve a healthy performance.

How to achieve that purpose:
- → Correct accounting and control procedure mistakes done previously.
- → Determine steps to be taken in order to improve performances based on the statement analysis.
- → Define the Motel's opportunities, weaknesses and pitfalls.
- → Relate this analysis to all previous analyses, and coordinate them in order to set strong guidelines to follow.

At this point, you should have a keen awareness of what is going on within and around the Motel that might influence any decision-making process. A clear outlook for 1996 should also be in your mind. This is the path to reach your goal.

★ Solution

Significant Difference Relative Balance Sheet to Statement of Income, 1996

Star Motel's statements of operations indicate a consistent amount depreciation and amortization over the years of $285,000. The balance sheets indicate that the amount should have been reduced to $270,000 because amortization of deferred charges came to an end at the end of 1994, leaving the historic amount of $285,000 - 15,000 = 270,000, (the $15,000 are the yearly amount of amortization of deferred charges). New fixed assets of $100,000 are projected to be added in 1996 which will have $15,000 annual depreciation. This results in total depreciation of $285,000.

Analysis

As these statements show, Star Motel will have a hard time during the first quarter or so of 1996 meeting its cash requirements because of unprofitable and unliquid situation following the negative result of 1995 operations. But if management procedures and control are followed, a great potential exists to radically reverse the situation in a very positive manner during a short period of time.

This potential can be summarized as follows:

- → Star Motel will be able to increase its net income from a negative $700,000 to a positive of $136,030 in 1996.
- → Cash could be increased by $678,900 in 1996, thus reversing the bad liquid situation to which it will be confined if adjustments are not made. This includes collection of the income tax refund.
- → Inventories and receivables must be decreased.
- → A reduction in current liabilities must be undertaken.
- → Working capital will be increased by $827,030 in 1996.

All of these statements point out the wide range of opportunities in which Star Motel operates. All it needs is a strong, efficient control system, a climate of trust in which management can operate, and an intelligent marketing plan that must be implemented as soon as possibly effective.

Star Motel has all of these strong opportunities from the outside, and it needs a strong reform from the inside; if things are done properly, success is just around the corner.

1996 is a very critical year for Star Motel. It is the year of changes. Star Motel must regain the trust of the community where it operates. It must show its good sense in doing business. Its tact and its reliability have to be proven in order to "repair its difficulties" in the inside and its challenges on the outside, always bearing in mind that a competitor is entering the same market at the beginning of 1997. That is why 1996 is the year where things must be decided.

The future market focus must be decided as the result of careful, concerned professional analysis.

Proper planning prevents poor performance.

Proper planning permits profit prosperity.

Section 14:

Capital Expenditures

★ Instruction

Capital Expenditures

Purpose:
To invest in the Motel's physical plan in order to increase revenue.

How to achieve that purpose:

- → Analyze the projected room demand for the area in order to determine the area's growth potential.
- → Analyze the projected meeting rooms demand for the area, and the Motel's present ability to meet this demand.
- → If the Motel cannot meet those future demands, determine what the cost of capital expenditures would be needed to accommodate those projected demands.
- → Determine the additional number of room demand based on capital expenditure.
- → Determine the additional number of meeting room demand based on capital expenditure.
- → Weigh the positives and negatives of these capital expenditures. For example, lost revenue, additional revenue, how does it affect the Motel's image and position, etc. . . . .
- → Draw a conclusion based on these findings, on whether or not to implement the changes.
- → Further improvements can be projected. For example, renovation. But because of the absence of data about the actual physical condition of the Motel, this will be left to your judgement.

★ Solution

Projected Meetings Room Demand For The Area				
Area	**1997**	**1998**	**1999**	**2000**
Industrial park (20-49 persons)	173	347	520	520
Research Center (80-100 persons)	—	—	104	104
Local Business (10-20 persons)	126	138	152	168
(30-40 persons)	189	208	228	251
(50 persons)	63	69	76	84
Total Demand (10-20 persons)	125	138	152	168
(21-50 persons)	425	624	824	855
(50-100 persons)	—	—	104	104

As we can see, meeting rooms demand in the area is expected to sharply increase in the coming years. The number of persons participating in each meeting varies from 10 to 100.

Star Motel's actual structure will be able to accommodate 10 to 20 persons meetings only. This portion on the total demand is very small. The Motel must strive to attract the other portion of the demand which falls into the range of 20 to 100 persons.

The projected demand, however, is expected to ask for more meeting rooms in the fifty to 100 persons range which Star Motel will not have the ability to provide.

As we already know, the availability of meeting rooms is one of the first reasons why businesses, groups and associations will come to the motel. Therefore, as an effective means to sell rooms and increase occupancy, Star Motel must do its best in order to accommodate these persons seeking meeting rooms, since it is guaranteed that a large portion of these people will stay in the Motel. Additionally, this would consolidate Star Motel's position as a place where people can meet.

In order to do so, store rental units which have a minimal income of $30,000 a year should be converted to a 100 seat meeting room. This meeting room should be divided into two 50-person rooms by using one removable sound proof panel.

★ Cost of Capital Expenditures

Removal of Walls	= $9,000 x 2	= $18,000
Sound Proof Panel		= $12,000
Other Improvements		= 300,000
Total Cost		$330,000

This capital investment should be implemented during January, 1997. Therefore, notice should be given to the store's operators as soon as possible in order to have them leave by December 31, 1996.

Other improvements might have to be done depending on the actual physical conditions of the Motel. Due to the lack of available information about these conditions, it is impossible for us to project any other improvement; an estimate of $300,000 is reasonable.

As stated earlier, the major competitor will be the new Holinite Inn. In order to compete effectively with a brand new property, Star Motel must make sure that the conditions of its facilities and furnishings are compatible with those of the Holinite Inn. A needs assessment program must be implemented showing the order of priorities for improvements based on needs. This program must be written and evaluated in 1996, and all the execution steps should be taken in 1997 where occupancy is expected to be lower that 1996.

Projected Additional Number of Meetings per Year Resulting from Capital Expenditures				
	1997	1998	1999	2000
21 - 50 persons	60	259	459	490
80 - 100 persons	—	—	104	104

These meetings will have an impact on generating revenue in all departments of the Motel. Revenue from the use of these meeting rooms will be generated. Food and beverages could be served causing a great impact on the food and beverage department. Rooms could be sold as a result of these meetings. Minor operating departments will benefit due to the great number of people using the facilities; the most important fact will be the Motel's ability to offer the services demanded by the segment of the business that Star Motel is going after.

At the same time, the room demand that is projected to take place in the coming years from the Industrial Park, the Research Center, and the local business visitor will most likely choose to stay at the Star Motel since their meetings will be held at the same place.

The lost revenue of $30,000 a year caused by converting the stores into meeting rooms does not at all match the potential revenues to be generated from this change. (The alternative to build new meeting rooms and keep the store rentals as they are should also be developed and may be a better alternative.)

Projected Room Demand Per Year Based on Capital Expenditures				
	1997	1998	1999	2000
Star Motel	51,281	55,188	59,860	66,211
Bay's Inn	19,447	21,864	28,113	29,036
Holinite Inn	29,171	33,958	40,515	41,610
Total Rooms Available Per Property Per Year				
Star Motel	73,000	73,000	73,000	73,000
Bay's Inn	36,500	36,500	36,500	36,500
Holinite Inn	54,750	54,750	54,750	54,750
Occupancy Percentage Per Property				
Star Motel	70.2%	75.6%	81.0%	90.7%
Bay's Inn	53.3%	59.9%	77.0%	80.0%
Holinite Inn	53.3%	62.0%	74.0%	76.0%

The assumptions leading to these figures are as follows:

→ As a result of concentrating marketing efforts on the meeting side of the business, Star Motel should be able to attract an average of 80% of its room demand coming from the Industrial Park, The Research Center, and the local business visitors.
→ This increased demand would allow increased room rates of an $8.00 spread as follows:
→ 1997—an increase of $2.00, bringing the average room rate to $44.00.
→ 1998—an increase of $2.00 bringing the average room rate to $46.00.
→ 1999—an increase of $2.00 bringing the average room rate to $48.00.
→ 2000—an increase of $2.00 bringing the average room rate to $50.00.
→ In addition to that, Star Motel must have its fair share from the highway demand, and the local demand.

Section 15:

Projected 5 Year Statement of Income With Increase Average Room Rate $2.00 Per Year

1996	No change
1997	$2.00 increase to $44.00
1998	$2.00 increase to $46.00
1999	$2.00 increase to $48.00
2000	$2.00 increase to $50.00

★ Instruction

Sales, Expenses, and Profit Forecast
1996, 1997, 1998, 1999, 2000

Purpose:
To prepare a projected statement of operations to be used as a measure of operational performances for 1996, 1997, 1998, 1999, 2000.

How to achieve that purpose:
The effects of the following have to be analyzed and translated into figures that will be used as projections for the coming five years.

- → Growth in the area demand (rooms, meeting rooms, food and beverages, and other departments).
- → Capital expenditures, (rooms, meeting rooms, food and beverages, and other departments).
- → Control and standards, (cost of sales in rooms, food and beverages, energy, and P.O.M.).
- → Labor cost control (payroll and related expenses in all departments).
- → Marketing plan (room sales, food and beverage sales, other incomes).

Standards should be able to justify every given figure based on their assumptions. These assumptions should be stated clearly and should be as realistic as possible.

★ Solution

Star Motel
Pro-Forma Comparative Statements of Operations
For The Year Ending December 31.

Page 1 of 2

Items	Amounts					Percentages (1)(2)				
	1996	1997	1998	1999	2000	1996	1997	1998	1999	2000
Rooms										
Sales	2,406,810	2,256,364	2,538,648	2,873,280	3,310,550	100.00%	100.00%	100.00%	100.00%	100.00%
Departmental Expenses										
Payroll and Related Expenses	376,666	301,532	346,220	373,526	397,266	15.65%	13.36%	13.64%	13.00%	12.00%
Other Expenses	164,385	107,690	123,650	129,998	137,000	6.83%	4.77%	4.87%	4.50%	4.14%
Total Expenses	541,051	409,222	469,870	502,824	534,266	22.48%	18.13%	18.51%	17.50%	16.14%
Departmental Income - Rooms	1,865,759	1,847,142	2,068,778	2,370,456	2,776,284	77.52%	81.87%	81.45%	82.50%	83.86%
Food and Beverage (1)										
Sales										
Food	1,440,000	1,262,853	1,436,814	1,751,259	2,030,000	71.43%	70.00%	70.00%	70.00%	70.00%
Beverage	576,000	541,222	615,778	750,539	870,000	28.57%	30.00%	30.00%	30.00%	30.00%
Total Sales	2,016,000	1,804,075	2,052,592	2,501,798	2,900,000	100.00%	100.00%	100.00%	100.00%	100.00%
Cost of Sales										
Food Cost	576,000	441,999	502,885	612,941	710,500	40.00%	35.00%	35.00%	35.00%	35.00%
Beverage Cost	144,000	119,069	135,471	165,119	191,400	25.00%	22.00%	22.00%	22.00%	22.00%
Total Costs	720,000	561,068	638,356	778,060	901,900	35.71%	31.10%	31.10%	31.10%	31.10%
Gross Profit	1,296,000	1,243,007	1,414,236	1,723,738	1,998,100	64.29%	68.90%	68.90%	68.90%	68.90%
Other Income - Net	60,000	63,143	76,972	112,581	174,000	2.98%	3.50%	3.75%	4.50%	6.00%
Gross Profit and Other Income	1,356,000	1,306,150	1,491,208	1,836,319	2,172,100	67.26%	72.40%	72.65%	73.40%	74.90%
Departmental Operating Expenses										
Payroll and Related Expenses	604,800	505,141	574,726	700,503	812,000	30.00%	28.00%	28.00%	28.00%	28.00%
Other Expenses	141,120	108,245	123,156	150,108	174,000	7.00%	6.00%	6.00%	6.00%	6.00%
Total Departmental Expenses	745,920	613,386	697,882	850,611	986,000	37.00%	34.00%	34.00%	34.00%	34.00%
Departmental Income - Food and Beverage	610,080	692,764	793,326	985,708	1,186,100	30.26%	38.40%	38.65%	39.40%	40.90%
Telephone [Loss]	<24,068>	<10,769>	12,365	45,213	90,000	1.00%	.48%	.49%	1.57%	2.72%
Minor Operating Departments	27,600	24,769	37,095	54,256	75,000	1.15%	1.10%	1.46%	1.89%	2.27%
Store Rentals	30,000	—	—	—	—	1.25%	—	—	—	—

Star Motel
Pro-Forma Comparative Statement of Operations
For the Years Ending December 31.

Items	Amounts					Percentages (1)(2)				
	1996	1997	1998	1999	2000	1996	1997	1998	1999	2000
Operated Departments										
Net Income	2,509,371	2,553,906	2,911,564	3,455,633	4,127,384	104.26%	113.19%	114.69%	120.27%	124.67%
Undistributed Operating Expenses										
Administrative and General										
Payroll and Related Expenses	168,477	107,690	123,650	129,298	138,000	7.00%	4.77%	4.87%	4.50%	4.17%
Other Expenses	216,613	150,766	173,110	181,017	191,000	9.00%	6.68%	6.82%	6.30%	5.78%
Total Administrative and General	385,090	258,456	296,760	310,315	329,000	16.00%	11.45%	11.69%	10.80%	9.94%
Marketing	240,681	172,304	148,380	150,000	150,000	10.00%	7.64%	5.84%	5.22%	4.53%
Energy	144,409	107,690	123,650	129,298	135,000	6.00%	4.77%	4.87%	4.50%	4.08%
P.O.M.	192,545	150,766	173,110	181,017	193,000	8.00%	6.68%	6.82%	6.30%	5.83%
Total Undistributed Operating Expenses	962,725	689,219	741,900	770,630	807,000	40.00%	30.55%	29.22%	26.82%	24.38%
Net Income Before Fixed Charges(3)	1,546,646	1,864,690	2,169,664	2,685,003	3,320,384	64.26%	82.64%	85.47%	93.44%	100.30%
Fixed Charges										
Municipal Taxes	192,545	180,509	203,092	214,800	264,844	8.00%	8.00%	8.00%	8.00%	8.00%
Insurance	120,341	86,152	98,920	114,000	128,000	5.00%	3.82%	3.90%	3.97%	3.87%
Total Taxes and Insurance	312,886	266,661	302,012	328,800	392,844	13.00%	11.82%	11.90%	11.44%	11.87%
Net Income Before Interest and Depreciation	1,233,760	1,598,029	1,867,652	2,356,203	2,927,540	51.26%	70.82%	73.57%	82.00%	88.43%
Interest Expense	722,043	701,000	701,000	701,000	701,000	30.00%	31.07%	27.61%	24.40%	21.17%
Net Income Before Depreciation	511,717	897,029	1,166,652	1,655,203	2,226,540	21.26%	39.76%	45.96%	57.61%	67.26%
Depreciation	270,000	270,000	270,000	270,000	270,000	11.22%	11.97%	10.64%	9.40%	8.16%
Net Income Before Tax	241,717	627,029	896,652	1,385,203	1,956,540	10.04%	27.79%	35.32%	48.21%	59.10%
Provision For Income Tax	96,687	250,812	358,661	554,081	782,616	4.02%	11.12%	14.13%	19.28%	23.64%
Net Income	145,030	376,217	537,991	831,122	1,173,924	6.03%	16.67%	21.19%	28.93%	35.46%

(1) Percentages are to room sales except food and beverage percentages are to food and beverage sales.
(2) Percentages may not add due to rounding.
(3) There are no management fees.

Section 16:

Conclusion

★ Instruction

Purpose:
To prepare a summary of the entire report.

How to achieve that purpose:
The problems future and actual problems are defined.
Improvements that should be implemented are stated.
The Motel's ultimate goals are defined.
Steps to achieve these goals are outlined.
Opportunities for expansion are concluded.
Short-term and long-term overview of Star Motel is provided.
Based on long-term projections, you should be able to recognize opportunities, and should be able to design a long-term action plan to achieve the best results.

★ Solution

The General Manager should outline his solutions and address the following:

As we have already mentioned, Star Motel has two major problems: the first can be detected through its declining occupancy; secondly, its inability to operate profitably.

Both problems could be solved if proper standards and procedures are implemented. An intelligent and effective marketing program must resolve the first problem. Control and policies in both staff and line departments must be able to solve the second problem.

Star Motel, if properly operated and managed, has the ability and potential to be one of the most profitable motels in the market. The area in which the Motel operates is a gold mine full of opportunities. Star Motel must know how and where to look for its business. The business meetings segment of the market is where Star Motel should be focusing. The Motel's facilities, after a few improvements, would be able to accommodate and attract almost 100% of the meetings segment of the businesses in that community; that is what Star Motel should strive for.

Management must also focus on the way operations are taking place. Goals must be set in all departments and must be reached. Service must improve, quality/value ratio must be felt by every guest, and control must be closely monitored.

If all the steps outlined in this report are followed, Star Motel should be able to reverse its unprofitable situation in 1996; it should be able to operate at a high occupancy and a high food and beverage turnover rate by 1999–2000. By then demand would warrant capitol expenditures to add at least 100 new rooms to the existing ones. Most of the capital would come from operations, and stockholders would be motivated to invest more and more capital back into the property. By then, creditors will also be interested in lending money since confidence would have been brought back in the way the Motel operates.

As the General Manager you have successfully undertaken a challenging job. Through learning first hand what was going on at the motel, evaluation of the personnel, developing a condensed business plan and marketing strategy you can now implement change with the support of the management team since they were key players in your evaluation process.

Enjoy your success—you have earned it.